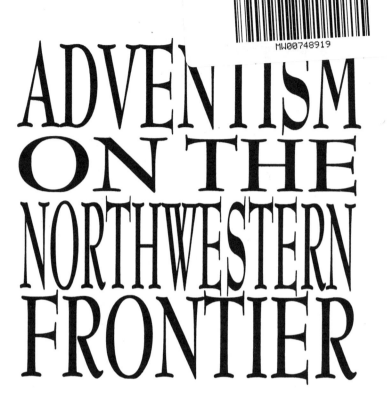

ADVENTISM ON THE NORTHWESTERN FRONTIER

ADVENTISM ON THE NORTHWESTERN FRONTIER

DOUG R. JOHNSON

ORONOKO BOOKS
BERRIEN SPRINGS, MI 49104-1700

To Richard and Arlene Johnson, my parents—
who loved me, sacrificed for me, and believed in me.

To Denise Johnson—my wife, my lover, and my friend.

To Hans and Erik—my sons and mountain-climbing buddies.

May we each stay close to Jesus Christ until He comes.

ISBN 1-883925-12-6
Library of Congress catalog card no. 96-067881

Printed in the United States of America
99 98 97 96   5 4 3 2 1

Contents

Foreword		vii
Preface		ix
1.	The Northwest's First Adventist	1
2.	He Couldn't Hide from the Sabbath	7
3.	A Missionary for the Northwest	13
4.	The Upper Country	21
5.	The Willamette Valley	27
6.	Ellen White Visits the Northwestern Frontier	37
7.	William Nichols	47
8.	New Leaders for the Northwest	53
9.	The Crisis of 1884	61
10.	The West Side	67
11.	Puget Sound	73
12.	The Inland Empire	79
13.	Father and Son	87
14.	Snake River Adventism	93
15.	Reading, Writing, and Arithmetic	99
16.	Conard Hall—The Rest of the Story	105
17.	Big Sky Country	109
18.	The Story Uncle Arthur Got Wrong	115
19.	Kellogg's Health System/Northwest	117
20.	The Germans and Scandinavians	121
21.	Evangelism in the Wild West	125
22.	Frontier Religion	131
Photographs		133
References		149
Notes		151

Foreword

Life, vitality, conflict, excitement, and human interest characterize Doug Johnson's *Adventism on the Northwestern Frontier*. It is a delightful book to read. (I dare you to read only one chapter.) The author moves us along at a brisk pace in a well-written, well-documented, high-interest account of the spread of Adventism in a sparsely populated but fast-growing part of the American frontier. With unusual perception he catches the essential feel and spirit of culture on that rambunctious frontier. He illustrates with clarity and charm how it was impacted when encountered by the advent message.

Opposition and the rise of dissident challenges seem to underline that Satan was hard on the heels of those who spread the message. "New light" urged by dissident members "almost made me have an ague chill," Ellen White complained while attending a camp meeting in the Upper Columbia Conference. Answering the challenge publicly, she reported the reaction to her very direct message as starting a "buzzing in the camp like a swarm of bees." (See page 62.)

Adventism on the Northwestern Frontier is not a handbook on evangelism, but the way members witnessed and won others to the faith is instructive and inspiring. It illumines the ways and spirit by which Adventism spread. Like a sweet potato that puts out a shoot at the end of which grows another potato that puts out more shoots on which other sweet potatoes grow, the church multiplied. One earnest Seventh-day Adventist who loved Jesus and believed He is coming again soon passed the good news on till another believed and then another and then others until there were a lot of Seventh-day Adventists. It was the sweet-potato-vine method and it worked.

The musty smell of canvas lingered in the nostrils of Seventh-day Adventist preachers as they proclaimed the advent message and appealed to sinners to come to Jesus. Building the kingdom was a front-burner priority for Seventh-day Adventists who either moved to the frontier or became members there. Churches multiplied and schools soon followed. This is a faith-inspiring reminder of our heritage.

Early entry into a small but growing population, recognition by church leadership that the greatest potential for growth was on the western frontier, praise, prayer, sacrifice, and a deep conviction that the Savior soon would come were keys to the successful spread of the church. Years have not changed the message or the hope of Seventh-day Adventists: Jesus is coming soon. The keys still turn locks and open doors.

Bruce Johnston, Former President
North Pacific Union Conference

Preface

By the end of the Civil War, land-hungry settlers snatched up most of the rich farmlands of the Midwest. This in turn forced newcomers into locating in either the semi-arid lands of the Great Plains or the rugged regions of the Wild West.

Those determined homesteaders who selected the Wild West entered a region unlike anything in the Midwest. They encountered a vast wilderness consisting of small valleys separated by desolate deserts, numerous mountain ranges and rolling grasslands.

Because of the Wild West's isolation from the rest of the nation, this western frontier developed into a colorful subculture that reflected its harsh surroundings. In recent years, Americans have become especially fascinated with this subculture. They are captivated by the exciting stories of the dangerous Oregon Trail, the bloody Indian wars, the rowdy gold rushes, and the rip-roaring cattle towns.

The primary purpose of *Adventism on the Northwestern Frontier* is to develop a readable yet thoroughly documented history of Adventism's encounter with the Northwestern frontier. The secondary purpose is to bring this history alive through human-interest stories, fascinating bits of secular and denominational history, and short, biographical sketches. The reader will meet a wealthy yet fanatical businessman, a resourceful and strong-willed pioneer, a spunky farmer's wife, a discouraged conference president, and many more early Northwestern Adventists.

However, *Adventism on the Northwestern Frontier* is not a collection of unsubstantiated stories viewed through the rosy glasses of a naive believer. It is a historical account based on four years of extensive research and is totally documented. The reader will find references for each chapter at the end of the book.

Though conceived in the northeastern corner of the United States, Sabbatarian Adventism soon developed into a frontier religion that moved westward with the men and women who settled the continent. In the 1860s, a few of these Adventists traveled to the remote frontiers of California, Oregon, and the Washington Territory. In time, these isolated believers began requesting ministerial help. The General Conference leaders responded by sending John N. Loughborough and Daniel T. Bourdeau to California in 1868 and Isaac D. Van Horn to the Washington Territory in 1874.

After establishing several churches in the Walla Walla Valley, Van Horn shifted his evangelistic efforts to the more populated Willamette Valley of western Oregon. In time, other Adventist ministers joined him and the denomination's presence in the Pacific Northwest grew. In the early 1880s, these ministers held tent meetings in the Palouse Hills and Puget Sound regions of Washington Territory and throughout western Oregon. During the next five years, they entered both Idaho and Montana Territories and launched several small academies. The 1890s saw continued growth in Northwestern Adventism and the beginnings of Walla Walla College and Portland Sanitarium. By the end of the century, the foundation of our present-day network of churches and institutions in the Pacific Northwest had been laid.

While much has been written about Adventism's early history in places like New England, Michigan and California, little has been recorded about the early work of the denomination in other regions of the country. Hence, many North American Adventists know little about their local religious heritage. In *Adventism on the Northwestern Frontier*, I have attempted to address this need for the believers of the Pacific Northwest.

1

The Northwest's First Adventist

Few places in the world and times in history hold as much fascination as the Wild West with its gunslinging cowboys, reckless gold miners, and determined pioneers. The drama of the Wild West builds on the excitement and uncertainty of its dangers. Legends and movies portray these tough settlers coping with wild animals, severe drought, cattle rustlers, and outlaws. But more than these, they picture the pioneers' courage in facing the region's native population.

The truth of the matter is that the first explorers and fur trappers were greeted by friendly Indians, not bloodthirsty savages. In 1804-06, the Lewis and Clark expedition was saved from starvation by the Nez Perce tribe and then safely guided to their destination—the Pacific Ocean.[1]

In the 1830s, a few hardy missionaries settled among these hospitable Indians and began teaching them about God. Though many of these nomadic people resisted this religious training and the civilized ways of the white man, most of them eagerly accepted his weapons and goods.

As large groups of determined pioneers began trudging across the Oregon Trail in the 1840s, the Cayuse Indians of eastern Oregon became alarmed. They were afraid that eventually these settlers would steal their land rather than continue to the Willamette Valley of western Oregon.

In 1847, the Cayuse Indians were exposed to measles while trading with a wagon train. The disease spread rapidly among them and developed into an epidemic which killed nearly half of the tribe. When the Indian leaders realized that the white people were not dying from the disease, their distrust of the whites turned to anger and then to hatred.

In November, the Cayuse Indians responded by attacking the Protestant mission in the Walla Walla Valley. They killed more than a dozen whites, including Dr. and Mrs. Marcus Whitman, and took captive 47 women and children. In time, fur traders from the Hudson Bay Company rescued the captives, but the remaining missionaries abandoned their Protestant missions and the government closed the country east of the Cascade Mountains to settlement.[2]

During the early 1850s, tensions between the white settlers and the Indians throughout the Northwest grew more and more intense. When the whites tried to force the Indians onto reservations in the mid-1850s, a general uprising took place. The United States Army, under the command of Colonel George Wright, responded promptly by crushing the "rebellion" and forcing the hostile tribes onto reservations.

With the Indians subdued, the government opened the eastern portions of Oregon and Washington Territory for settlement. Because Fort Walla Walla was the region's only military post, the Walla Walla Valley became the hub of this new frontier.[3]

Among the earliest settlers in the Northwest region was Augusta Moorhouse, a Seventh-day Adventist, and her husband Thomas, a non-Adventist. This middle-aged couple traveled over the rugged Oregon Trail to this frontier with their eight children. Now, why would a well-established farmer like Thomas Moorhouse leave the comfort and safety of an Iowa farm for an uncertain future in a remote and dangerous frontier? Why would he subject his family to the extremely dangerous trip across the Oregon Trail and then settle them in a region with hostile Indians? To answer these questions, one must look at the events that took place prior to their trip west.[4]

In the summer of 1859, two Adventist ministers, Merritt E. Cornell and Moses Hull, brought a large tent to Knoxville, Iowa. As soon as the preachers erected the canvas meeting house, gossipers began spreading the rumor that they were Mormon polygamists. Instead of keeping the town folk away from the tent meetings, the rumor aroused interest. Between six and eight hundred attended the evangelistic meetings each evening. After several months, fifty of these curiosity seekers accepted the Adventist message and formed a church that soon grew to a membership of one hundred.[5]

One of those who listened and embraced Adventism was Augusta Moorhouse. Augusta was born in Germany, and came to Iowa when only a child. In time, she fell in love and married Thomas Moorhouse.[6]

Soon after Auguta joined the Adventist church, James and Ellen White arrived in Knoxville in March 1860 to encourage the new believers who made up the largest group of Sabbath-keeping Adventists west of the Mississippi River. As the Whites approached Knoxville, the rumor that they were Mormon polygamists surfaced again. A few residents even wanted to tar and feather them! However, after listening to the Whites speak in the courthouse, the people calmed down. As the meetings continued, the crowd grew so large that windows had to be removed from the courthouse so that the people outside could hear.[7]

Thomas Moorhouse was a temperamental man. He cared very little for his wife's Adventism. In fact, he was so upset that in 1861 he pulled up stakes from where he had farmed for nearly twenty years and moved his family by ox-drawn wagon to the newly opened frontier of the Walla Walla Valley in Washington Territory.[8]

Thomas selected a homestead of 160 acres about eight miles south of Walla Walla at the base of the Blue Mountains.[9] He thought that if he located his family in this remote region, he would isolate them from almost everyone. And he was right! So far as we know, Augusta was the only Adventist in the Northwest at that time.

Thomas misjudged the determination of his German wife. Though isolated, Augusta remained true to her beliefs. She faithfully read her Bible and kept in touch with her church through the *Review and Herald*. Augusta quickly learned that life on the western frontier was vastly different from life in Iowa. Instead of being surrounded by endless farmland, she was confronted with an untamed wilderness dominated by rough men, wild animals, and Indians. This land, with its scattered farms and towns, only vaguely resembled the civilization she had known.

The year before the Moorhouses arrived in the Walla Walla Valley, gold was discovered in what soon became the Idaho Territory. In 1861 the precious metal was also found in eastern Oregon. These discoveries brought thousands of men seeking their fortune, and Walla Walla became the supply center for these gold fields. As a result, the settlement mushroomed from a quiet village of a few buildings to the largest town in the Washington Territory.

Shortly after the Moorhouses arrived in the Northwest, two of their sons succumbed to gold fever. In 1864, Darius and his younger brother Lee (15 years old) convinced their parents that they were old enough to go in search of the hidden bonanza. Augusta must have shed many a tear as she saw her boys ride away, for she knew that the gold districts were dangerous, immoral places that harbored ruthless outlaws, gamblers, and prostitutes.

The boys tried prospecting in Idaho Territory first, but the yellow metal eluded them. Next, they traveled north to the gold fields of British Columbia. After several years of hard work in Canada, the glamor of gold mining evaporated and they returned home poorer and probably wiser than they had left.[10] Later in life, Lee became a photographer of Indian life. In 1906 he published a book of Indian photographs.[11] One of these won him international recognition and it still hangs in the Smithsonian Institute in Washington, D. C. Lee also served as mayor of Pendleton, was the superintendent of the Umatilla Indian Reservation, and, for twenty-five years, was the clerk of the Oregon Supreme Court.[12]

For seven years on the western frontier, Augusta never saw another Seventh-day Adventist, but she did not let this isolation shake her young faith. In 1868, she wrote a letter to the *Review and Herald*:

> Your cheering testimonies encourage me to press forward with renewed zeal toward the kingdom of God. I desire to give my testimony in behalf of the truth of the third angel's message and for the *Review*. I am trying to keep the commandments of God with all my heart. If I can say at last that I have fought a good fight, I have kept the faith . . . it will be enough.[13]

In time Augusta made friends with a Seventh Day Baptist family, the Stephen Maxsons, who lived several miles from her home. Their story and the beginnings of Adventism in the Walla Walla Valley will be told in the next chapter.

In 1882, Thomas and Augusta purchased a farm east of Weston, Oregon.[14] Augusta died in 1903. On her tombstone in the Weston cemetery is written:

Revelation 14:12, Here is the patience of the saints: here are they that keep the commandments of God, and the faith of Jesus.

2
He Couldn't Hide from the Sabbath

During the 1800s, the western frontier tempted thousands of Americans with the promise of unlimited opportunities and free land. Some were lured to the edges of civilization by the excitement of living in an untamed wilderness; others were drawn to the western frontier in hopes of building a better future.

Soon after their marriage in 1837, Stephen and Lois Maxson, Seventh Day Baptists, became fascinated by the possibilities of the Wisconsin frontier. Being young and energetic, the newlyweds decided to leave their home in New York state and take their chances out West.

Soon the Maxsons, like other settlers, discovered that Wisconsin's harsh winters and thin soil made the raising of wheat a risky business. When the western lands with their richer soils began opening up about twenty years later, the Maxsons were ready for a change. They packed their few belongings and headed for the frontier of Nebraska. Again, as in Wisconsin, they were not satisfied. They longed for something better.[1]

In 1859, news of the Pikes Peak gold rush hit the western frontier like a tornado. Thousands of unhappy settlers itching for a change pulled up stakes and headed for the Rockies. Since the Maxsons and their daughter's family, the Woods, yearned for a more ideal frontier in which to build their future, they purchased oxen and wagons and joined the mass exodus. Only a hundred miles from their destination, they learned that the gold rush had played out. Discouraged by the bad news, they changed their course for yet another frontier—the Walla Walla Valley in Washington Territory.[2]

Stephen Maxson was elected captain of their wagon train and had the heavy responsibility of coordinating the movements of nearly a hundred wagons. At one point in their six-month journey, an Indian chief offered to purchase the Maxson's fourteen-year-old daughter Lucy, a pretty girl with blue eyes and long curly hair. Of course, Stephen refused to sell her, but the chief continued to follow the wagon train, offering more furs and more ponies. Finally, after six days, the Indian leader got the message that Lucy was not for sale and ceased his pursuit.

Along the Platte River, one of the men spied a white paper fluttering from a buffalo skull—a message warning travelers that the Indians would try to stampede and capture their animals. As predicted, the Indians came at midnight and began riding around and around the circle of wagons, but all the men and boys in Maxson's wagon train were armed and on the alert, and soon the Indians rode away without either side firing a shot.[3] At one river crossing, Stephen was swept away by the swift current. Men from the wagon train found him half a mile downstream clutching to a branch and nearly unconscious.

The grueling trip across the Oregon Trail tried the patience and endurance of all. Supplies ran short. Oxen died of exhaustion. Indians stole livestock. Sickness plagued nearly every family. When the bone-weary group finally spied the Walla Walla Valley from the Blue Mountains, they stopped the wagon train, took down the Maxson's precious melodeon, and sang several songs of praise.[4]

The Maxsons and Woods arrived in the Walla Walla Valley just as the area was opened for settlement after the recently concluded Indian wars. Walla Walla at that time consisted of a military fort, "two log houses, one store, a law office and a few scattered settlers."[5] The Maxsons and Woods homesteaded on Russell Creek about seven miles southeast of Walla Walla. The house Stephen built is still standing.[6]

In 1862, the elected leaders of the Walla Walla Valley settlements decided to bring some culture to the frontier. They appointed James Franklin Wood, Maxson's son-in-law, as the superintendent of public schools. At that time, the only public schools in the Northwest were in the Willamette Valley of western Oregon.

The first public schoolhouse erected east of the Cascade Mountains was on land donated by Stephen Maxson. It was called the Maxson schoolhouse. By 1864, Wood had established twelve school districts in the Walla Walla Valley. Seven of these districts built schoolhouses.[7]

Stephen Maxson's daughter, Caroline Wood, excelled in music. In 1867, Maxson ordered a rosewood piano from the Hallet Davis Company of Boston. The piano was shipped around the southern tip of South America and up the Columbia River to Wallula. There, a wagon hauled the precious instrument over bumpy roads to the Wood's homestead on Russell Creek. For many years it was the only piano in the Walla Walla Valley.[8]

Caroline had a beautiful voice, so she was invited to sing on a regular basis for the soldiers at Fort Walla Walla. The pioneers of the region called her "Jenny Lind of the West." When U.S. President Rutherford B. Hayes visited the Walla Walla Valley in 1880, Caroline sang for the gathering.[9]

When Maxson's son, Samuel, and son-in-law, James Franklin Wood, arrived in the area, they wanted nothing to do with religion. But years later, both men and their families experienced conversion during a revival conducted by a minister from the United Brethren Church. As a result, they built a small church on Wood's property and became zealous members of the Brethren Church. Stephen Maxson and his wife who were still Seventh Day Baptists also worshiped with this church. Stephen even accepted the position as a class leader with the understanding that he and his wife would also keep the seventh-day Sabbath.

One day, Augusta Moorhouse learned that the Maxson family also observed the Sabbath. Excited about the possibility of fellowshiping with another Sabbath-keeping family in the remote frontier, she saddled her horse and rode over to their farm. During her visit, Augusta introduced the Maxsons to the *Review and Herald* and asked them why they were going to church on Sunday. Because of Augusta's straightforward questioning, the Maxsons decided to stop attending the Brethren Church. James Wood was outraged when he learned of this change by his inlaws. Augusta continued visiting the Maxsons to share her faith. Wood, who had heard enough of Augusta and the Sabbath issue, was so irritated that he moved his family to a rented farm in Windsor, California to escape the doctrines.

By 1868, nearly half a million people resided in California. Only about fifty were Seventh-day Adventists. Providentially, James Wood moved next door to one of them—William Nichols.

Coincidentally, it was just at this time that John N. Loughborough and Daniel T. Bourdeau, the first Adventist ministers to preach west of the Rocky Mountains, arrived in California to hold evangelistic meetings in Petaluma and Windsor. When William Nichols invited Wood to the Windsor meetings, Wood decided to attend.[10]

Loughborough and Bourdeau experienced success on the West Coast. Within five years, they established seven churches with 238 members in this isolated mission field.[11]

Several months later Wood accepted the Adventist message and was baptized during the first Seventh-day Adventist baptism in California on April 11, 1869. He was so excited about Adventism that he sold his unharvested crops. With the income from the sale, he moved his family back to the Walla Walla Valley. Here he accepted a teaching position for the Maxson public school, meanwhile sharing his new beliefs with his friends and relatives. After several months, the Stephen Maxsons joined Augusta Moorhouse and the Woods to form the first group of Seventh-day Adventists in the Pacific Northwest.[12] Also joining this group was the Maxson's youngest daughter, Frances Coston, and her husband, Seneca, who was a minister with the United Brethren Church. Several years later the Costons moved from the Walla Walla Valley.[13]

When Wood left California, he brought with him a prophetic chart and a supply of Adventist literature. On Sunday evenings, he conducted meetings in the Maxson schoolhouse, an activity that caused strong opposition among the local clergy. Wood claimed that his lectures caused these ministers to squirm, but it appears that no one outside his own family joined the Adventist group.

During the autumn of 1869, Wood and Maxson sent $27.00 to the Review and Herald Publishing Association in Battle Creek, Michigan, for additional books and pamphlets for distribution. By 1873 several individuals had joined the growing Adventist group in the Walla Walla Valley through their outreach efforts.[14]

The James Bunch family, more Adventists, moved to the Walla

Walla Valley in 1871 and located about five miles southeast of what is now Milton-Freewater. Two years earlier, someone had sent a bundle of *Review and Herald*s to their Missouri home and the Bunches accepted the Adventist message. They moved to California in 1869 but soon relocated in the Northwest.[15]

After returning to the Northwest, Wood wrote two of his Adventist friends in California to encourage them to move to the beautiful Walla Walla Valley. William Nichols and (Aaron Miller) responded bringing their families north in covered wagons and settling near Milton-Freewater.[16]

For several years, the scattered Adventist believers worshiped together on a monthly basis. Minnie Ford wrote of one of these religious gatherings:

> There were two seasons of prayer and praise and testimonies, interspersed with a lunch for everybody at noon. The Holy Spirit was present and there was joy and gladness, and a refreshing from the presence of the Lord.[17]

As the Adventist group in the Walla Walla Valley continued to grow, it became apparent that some form of organization was needed. In April 1873, these believers formed the First Seventh-day Adventist Church of Walla Walla. Stephen Maxson wrote:

> Elder Coston preached two feeling sermons on Sabbath, with a conference meeting. The Lord was in our midst, and that to bless. He also preached two sermons on the first day. After the first sermon, we organized a church of nineteen members. Elected S. S. Coston for our minister; S. Maxson was chosen and ordained for deacon; J. F. Wood, church clerk. . . . Then we retired to the river, and with singing and prayers and tears witnessed the baptism of six young converts. Returned to the house; heard a sermon on the near coming of Christ; after which a social meeting.

Soon after Wood's return to the Northwest, the few believers in the Walla Walla Valley began requesting a minister. Since they lived nearly 1000 miles from the nearest Adventist church or preacher, they felt that an Adventist minister should be assigned to their region.

Hoping to speed up the arrival of a preacher, they sent money to Merritt E. Cornell in California, but he returned it. Their hopes rose in 1872 when they received word that Cornell would soon visit the Northwest. Unfortunately nothing happened.[18]

In the 22 July 1873 issue of the *Review and Herald*, John N. Loughborough, president of the California Conference, reported that Merritt E. Cornell would start a mission in the Northwest after the California camp meeting. One month later, he changed his mind and announced that the General Conference would handle the starting of a mission in the Northwestern frontier. The news of another delay must have come as a great disappointment to those isolated believers who already had waited four years for an Adventist preacher.[19]

3
A Missionary for the Northwest

In 1873, the General Conference responded to the requests for a minister in the Pacific Northwest by sending Isaac and Adelia Van Horn to the region.

Joseph Bates introduced Isaac, a school teacher near Jackson, Michigan, to Adventism 14 years earlier. After only two sermons, Isaac had accepted the Sabbath.

Four years later, he started ministerial work and was soon ordained. His first years in the ministry were spent helping veteran ministers hold tent meetings in Michigan.

In 1865, Isaac married Adelia Patten who was living with the James White family and assisting Ellen with her writing. During their first years of marriage, Isaac worked as the treasurer of the General Conference while Adelia served as the editor of the *Youth's Instructor*.[1]

The Van Horns traveled to California in December 1873 over the newly constructed transcontinental railroad. After spending the winter working with the believers in California, they boarded an ocean steamer in San Francisco for Portland, Oregon, where they transferred to a steamboat for the trip up the Columbia River. In the early 1870s, steamboats and stagecoaches served as the main forms of public transportation in the northwestern frontier.[2]

The need for a mission in the Pacific Northwest had been presented to the members of the young Seventh-day Adventist Church in the pages of the *Review and Herald*. Over 100 individuals, whose names were printed in the *Review*, responded to the challenge. Their donations made it possible for the small denomination of around 7,000 members to send the Van Horns and their tent to the Northwest.[3]

James F. Wood met the Van Horns at the steamboat dock in Wallula and took them and their 60-foot tent to Walla Walla. The 30-mile ride must have been especially difficult for Adelia who was pregnant with her first child and suffering from "weak lungs."[4]

In a letter to James and Ellen White, Adelia described the small group of Adventists they found in the Walla Walla area.

Brother [James F.] Wood['s family] is the only Sabbath keeping family in the city. Father [Stephen] Maxson living seven miles out is the nearest one to the town, and the rest are scattered from seven to thirty miles distant. At our first meeting I was particularly struck with their plain appearance. The brethren did not have on broadcloth and white collars, but rather coarse gray and blue, and heavy boots, and the sisters were accordingly plain. But their testimonies seemed to come from warm hearts, and before the meeting was out I loved them all.

In her letter, Adelia also pointed out that at present none of the Walla Walla believers were able to become involved in full-time ministry. Describing the two best candidates, she wrote:

Brother Wood has raised an interest every place where he has held meetings. He holds back from the ministry on account of having a large family of 7 children to support. He is in debt—though once in good circumstances. . . . Brother [Seneca] Coston is also son-in-law of Brother Maxson. He has been a United Brethren preacher. I don't know how long he has been an Adventist, but he does not understand our doctrines well enough to preach them. He has 5 little children. His health is not very good—having violent attacks of sick-headache often—has no property of any account. . . . We hope he might 'courage up,' and make a stir.[5]

Soon after arriving in Walla Walla, the largest town in Washington Territory with a population of about 2,000, Van Horn looked for a location to set up the tent. Finally, he found a French Catholic, Toussaint ("Charlie") Chabot, who agreed to let him erect the tent near his vineyard at the corner of Fourth and Birch, believing that he might earn some merits with God by doing this good deed.

Because of his Catholic convictions, Charlie at first would not attend the meetings; however, he enjoyed sitting on his porch and listening to the good music.

During his sermons, Van Horn spoke loudly hoping Charlie would hear. He did, and he liked what he heard! So each evening he moved his chair a little closer to the canvas meeting house. Finally, Charlie joined the group inside the tent. At the end of the meetings he became a member of the Adventist church and donated the lot where the tent had been pitched as a future site for a church building.[6] Charlie Chabot loved music. After the Walla Walla church erected a building, he always sat on the front pew by the organ. Even though he couldn't carry a tune, he still sang enthusiastically, which bothered some of the members.

One day after church the disgruntled members approached the organist, Caroline Wood, noted as the best musician in the Walla Walla Valley, asking her to visit with Charlie about his loud singing. Caroline replied: "Not for anything would I hurt his feelings. Let Brother Chabot sing. He enjoys it. The Lord knows all about the motive that prompts him to want to sing praises."[7]

On May 12, Van Horn sent in a report of the meetings.

Our meetings have now been in progress nineteen days. . . . Last Sunday evening, the 10th, after giving a discourse on the restoration of the Bible Sabbath, we called upon all of those who were convinced that the seventh day was the Bible Sabbath, to manifest it by rising to their feet. Between fifty and seventy-five immediately got up. . . . There were about three hundred and fifty present at the meeting.[8]

Van Horn baptized four individuals on May 17 in Mill Creek and officially organized the group of 35 believers as the Walla Walla Seventh-day Adventist Church.[9] One of the individuals who joined this church that summer was Alonzo T. Jones. Adelia Van Horn described him as

A young man, a soldier from the garrison (Fort Walla Walla). For weeks he has been earnestly seeking the Lord, and a few days since received bright evidences of sins forgiven. After being buried with Christ (baptized) he arose exclaiming with upraised hands, 'Dead to the world, and alive to thee, O my God.'[10]

During the next year, while in the military, Jones spent his spare time studying the Bible, especially the prophecies. As a result, he gained a solid knowledge of the Scriptures. In July 1875, the Walla Walla Church asked the General Conference leaders to give Jones a license to preach. When he was discharged from the military in November 1875, Jones began full-time ministerial work by helping Van Horn hold evangelistic meetings.[11]

Jones had left his home in Rockhill, Ohio, at the age of 20, and had enlisted in the United States Army where he served for five years. After two years in the Southwest, Jones' regiment was transferred to Fort Vancouver in the Northwest.

By the 1870s, most western Indian tribes had been forced by the military to locate on small reservations, but in northern California, a group of 50 Modoc Indians refused to stay on their reservation. When troops had been sent in against them in 1872, the rebellious Indians hid among the lava beds near Tule Lake. Here they boasted that they could withstand a thousand soldiers.

After an unsuccessful attempt to force the Modocs from their fortress, the military leaders realized that they needed additional troops. In the lava beds, nine soldiers had been killed and 30 wounded without their ever seeing an Indian. The soldiers' shoes and clothing also had been shredded by the sharp volcanic rocks.

In January of 1873, Alonzo Jones' company traveled to the end of the railroad line in Roseburg, Oregon, and marched over the mountains to the battlefield. At this point the government decided to send a peace commission to the renegade Indians. At the meeting, while one group of Modocs was attacking the commissioners, another group approached the soldiers on the east side of the lava beds under a flag of truce. When Lieutenants Sherwood and Boyle ventured out to talk, the Indians opened fire. As they scrambled for safety, Sherwood was mortally wounded, but Boyle escaped.

In later years, Alonzo Jones, whose squad was the closest to the shooting, wrote: "It has always been one of the supremest satisfactions of my life that by pouring in a hail of bullets beyond where the wounded officer [Sherwood] lay, my squad was able effectually to prevent any further savagery being perpetuated upon him and so to protect him till he could be carried to camp." Because of the aggressive response by Jones' squad, Lieutenant Boyle was able to run to safety and the Modocs were prevented from scalping Lieutenant Sherwood.

In retaliation, soldiers attacked the Modocs' volcanic stronghold. Jones wrote: "I was in and through the fight of three nights and days that drove the Modocs out of their stronghold. It was the good fortune of my squad to get between the stronghold and the lake, so as to shut them off from water and compel them to abandon the place."

When the Modocs were captured, Jones' company escorted them to Fort Klamath in Oregon. There, four Indian leaders were hanged for killing the commissioners. The rest of the Modocs were taken to Indian Territory (known today as Oklahoma).

After completing their duties at Fort Klamath, the soldiers in Jones' company were assigned to Fort Walla Walla. Through the middle of the summer, these battle-weary soldiers marched across the desert of eastern Oregon. Not much of a reward for war duty![12]

In 1874, Van Horn was experiencing success in his ministry. In fact, other ministers in Walla Walla began preaching against Adventist doctrines; however, this did not stop the people from attending Van Horn's tent meetings.[13] By June, Van Horn wrote: "We are told that we have already the largest church in the place except the Catholic."[14]

The tent meetings continued to meet with tremendous success. By 1875 the Walla Walla SDA Church had over 60 members and a new church building (32' x 46') that cost nearly $3,000.[15] At the time, it was one of the nicest church structures in Walla Walla. Van Horn quoted the local newspaper, *The Walla Walla Statesman*, that described it as "the best house of worship in Oregon and Washington Territory, except one, east of the Cascade Mountains."[16]

In a report to the *Signs of the Times*, James F. Wood conveyed the excitement of the Walla Walla believers.

The work is gaining ground all the time. We have a beautiful house of worship nearly completed. . . . The people here are astonished that we have pushed the enterprise through so successfully. It has arisen, as if by magic.[17]

In September of 1874, Van Horn erected his tent in Weston, Oregon, where he baptized the William Russell family. Next, he moved his tent to Milton, Oregon, a village of 50 inhabitants. Here, he was able to organize a Sabbath school of 15 members led by Aaron Miller and William Nichols.[18]

In early 1875, Van Horn turned his efforts to Pendleton, Oregon, a village of 200 inhabitants and the county seat. Later he went to Waitsburg in Washington Territory. At both these locations he met with minimal results.[19]

The original plan of the General Conference was for Van Horn to spend one year in the remote Walla Walla Valley and then move to the more populated Willamette Valley. Since in April, it was announced in the *Review and Herald* that Elbert B. Lane would be coming to the Northwest, Van Horn decided to wait for him in the Walla Walla Valley. Besides, Adelia, who had given birth to a son in November, was still struggling with poor health and was in no condition to move.

In June, Van Horn set up his tent in Dayton, a village of 300 inhabitants in Washington Territory; attendance ran between 100 and 250. At the end of these meetings, he organized a small Sabbath school of 16 members.[20]

In August, Van Horn sent a report to the General Conference summarizing his work for the past 16 months.

When we arrived in the Walla Walla Valley, we found about thirty keeping the Sabbath, and a church of eighteen members partially organized. . . . Since that first meeting, we have pitched the tent in five places with some believers as the result in each place. The number of Sabbath-keepers has been increased to about one hundred. . . . A meeting-house has been built in Walla Walla, costing $3000. . . . There are two men who have proved themselves of sufficient ability to present the truth in an acceptable manner . . . Brother J. F. Wood and Brother A. T. Jones, a young soldier . . . stationed in Fort Walla Walla.[21]

After holding meetings east of the Blue Mountains in La Grande, Oregon, Van Horn spent the winter working with the believers in the Walla Walla Valley. In January, he organized the 17 members in Milton as a church, and several months later organized a church in Dayton, the third church in the Northwest.[22]

With the work well established in the Walla Walla Valley, Van Horn and his new assistant, Alonzo T. Jones, boarded the steamboat at Wallula in early May of 1876, and traveled to the Willamette Valley of western Oregon.[23]

4
The Upper Country

From the 1850s through the 1870s, the territory between the Cascade and Rocky Mountain Ranges including the Walla Walla Valley was known as the "Upper Country." The name probably came from the fact that this inland region was farther up the Columbia River than the Willamette Valley.

After Van Horn and Jones left the Upper Country in 1876, Joseph Waggoner traveled to the Northwest from California and spent three months helping in the region. During his stay, he visited the Upper Country and reported that Stephen Maxson had sold his farm and had moved into Walla Walla so he could spend more time nurturing the young Walla Walla Church.[1] The next year, Maxson was given a ministerial license; and in 1879, his son-in-law, James Wood, also received a license to preach.[2]

Soon after Waggoner left the Walla Walla Valley, a serious situation developed for the believers of the Upper Country. One of the members of the newly formed Milton Church was a farmer named William Goodwin who had moved his family to the Walla Walla Valley in 1871. He purchased 80 acres along the Walla Walla River just north of Milton. In 1875, the family attended Van Horn's tent meetings and joined the Adventist Church.[3]

One day, William Goodwin was picking pears in his orchard. As he reached for a pear, his foot slipped and he fell to the ground, landing on his neck and injuring his spinal column. Several hours later, he recovered enough to return to work. About six weeks after the accident, William began showing signs of mental instability. His distressed family took him to the doctor in Walla Walla. He told the family that William had "a regular case of insanity." He also explained to them that William would either die or remain insane for the rest of his life.

Soon, almost everyone in the valley began shunning the Adventists, those people with the crazy religion.

The report in the *Signs of the Times* stated, "People were more ready to believe this report than the truth in his case. Our brethren both in Milton and Walla Walla began to feel the blow heavily."

At William Goodwin's request, the elders of the Milton and Walla Walla churches came to his home for a special season of prayer. The report in the *Signs of the Times* stated:

> From that hour Brother Goodwin began to get better. In about two weeks he went into the city and greatly surprised the doctor as he stepped into his office to settle his bill. His restoration was a wonder to all, but a great joy to the friends of present truth.[4]

After being away from the Walla Walla Valley for an entire year, Van Horn visited the region in March of 1877. He found a good spirit in the Walla Walla and Milton churches, but the Dayton congregation was a different situation. To help them solve their problems, Van Horn conducted 11 meetings and reported that "good feelings [were] restored among them."[5]

In October, John N. Loughborough, president of the California Conference, along with Van Horn and Jones traveled to Walla Walla for the organization of the North Pacific Conference. With a total of five churches and 200 members, the General Conference felt that the Northwestern believers were strong enough to be financially "self-sustaining." Thirty years later, Loughborough described his trip from Portland to Walla Walla.

> The trip was a real contrast to present-day travel. We left Portland by boat [steamboat] at 5 a.m., Monday, and sailed to the Cascades. Then all the freight was carried on men's shoulders to a train that went three miles on the north side of the river around the Cascades, to the old block fort of [President] Grant's time. There we waited until 4 p.m. while the freight was carried to a second steamer [steamboat]. At 11 p.m. we reached The Dalles where we boarded another train which took us around The Dalles to Celio. At 4 a.m. all the freight was transferred to another steamer [steamboat] taking

us to Wallula where we spent the night. At 9 a.m., Wednesday, we took passage on Dr. Baker's railroad reaching Walla Walla after 55 hours from Portland.[6]

At the session, Isaac D. Van Horn was elected president of the new conference with his wife as secretary and Alonzo T. Jones as treasurer. The delegates to the session also voted to adopt the quarterly meeting system recommended by the General Conference and to support the newly established Pacific Press in California by purchasing stock. The resolution concerning the quarterly meetings read thus:

A quarterly meeting [should be held] in each church on the first Sabbath and Sunday of each quarter. A district quarterly meeting in each district, the second Sabbath and Sunday in each quarter and a state quarterly meeting on the third Sabbath and Sunday in each quarter.[7]

During the summer of 1877, the members of the Milton Church erected a small church building on Main Street. In 1880, the Dayton congregation also put up a structure, 24 by 36 feet, at the corner of Guernsey and Fourth Streets. This building is no longer used as an Adventist church, but it is the oldest Adventist-built structure still standing in the Pacific Northwest.[8]

During the summer of 1878, a diphtheria epidemic swept through the Walla Walla Valley. It hit James F. Wood's home especially hard. Three of their seven children died. Caroline became so upset over the ordeal that she almost lost her sanity.

When Ellen White heard the shocking news, she wrote to the family and encouraged Caroline to spend a year in Battle Creek, Michigan. To escape the scene of her terrible loss and to provide some educational benefits for her family, Caroline took White's advice. After traveling to Battle Creek, she enrolled three of the children in the denomination's only college and placed Rufus in the Battle Creek Sanitarium to correct a limb deformity.

The next summer, Caroline left Minnie at the college and brought the three boys home.[9] Several months later, she experienced another loss when her father, Stephen Maxson, passed away.[10]

While Caroline was in Michigan, Ellen White counseled her to have more children. In time, the Woods had two more girls, Grace and Edith. These girls were always referred to as "the second crop."

A few years later (1883) when James F. Wood found himself in failing health, the Woods moved to Medical Lake in Washington Territory to be near the famed baths that reportedly had medicinal properties. There James worked in the hotel business.[11]

Though the Woods had gone through some difficult times in the late 1870s, they remained faithful to God and their little church in Walla Walla. James continued to serve as an elder and trustee, while Caroline helped with the music. After their move to Medical Lake, the Woods became very casual about their Sabbath observance. Early in 1884, the Walla Walla Church responded by placing them under censure. Several months later, the Woods asked the church to drop their names from the membership list. The church did so in early 1885 "for not living up to the rules of the church."[12]

Four months later, John N. Loughborough visited the scattered believers in the Palouse Hills of Washington Territory. One of his stops was at the Wood's home in Medical Lake. Before he left, they "promised to fully obey the truth."[13] In 1887, the Wood's son-in-law, Clarence Ford, spent several months holding evangelistic meetings in Medical Lake. The following year a small church was organized in the town.[14]

James Wood's health continued to deteriorate and late in 1894, he passed away. Two days before his death, James wrote a letter to his family. In part he stated:

> I feel that my life has been of very little good, [I] have made many mistakes, have not set the example before you that I should have done. . . . I can now only ask His forgiveness and yours, and hope that you will realize more fully than ever that our time here is short at most. And we should do all we can to be ready to meet Jesus at his coming. Herewithstanding [sic] all my imperfections and sins which are many. I go down into the dust in full faith that Jesus is my Saviour and that He will redeem me from the grave when He comes with all power and glory.[15]

In the summer of the diphtheria epidemic in Walla Walla (1878) when three of the Wood's children died, the United States Army was fighting a war with the Bannock Indians in southern Idaho Territory and eastern Oregon. When Van Horn learned of this development, he considered canceling his visit to the Upper Country, but he finally decided to make the trip. When he arrived at the Walla Walla church he found it in mourning for the Wood's children, and he heard that the Milton Church was struggling with a "severe trial." After working with these two churches, Van Horn and his assistant William Raymond erected the conference's new 50 foot tent in Dayton and held a series of meetings. Next, they moved the tent to the small village of Pataha, near present-day Pomeroy; there 10 individuals accepted the Adventist message. The next year a small church was organized in Pataha.[16]

In his report to the *Signs of the Times*, Van Horn indicated that many of the Walla Walla members lived long distances from the church and, as a result, the church was beginning to struggle. He ended his report by stating: "Let no one think that the cause is dead in this church. Far from it."[17]

During the summer of 1879, Stephen Haskell, president of the California Conference, along with Van Horn and his two assistants, conducted a camp meeting about five miles east of Walla Walla. It was the denomination's first camp meeting in the Upper Country. About 230 attended the gathering which was held in a grove of cottonwood trees along Mill Creek.[18] At this camp meeting, the independent-minded members of the Upper Country tried to form a separate conference for the territory east of the Cascade Mountains. After an "animated discussion," a motion was made to petition the General Conference for the authority to form a new organization to be known as the "Walla Walla Conference." Haskell and Van Horn urged the delegates to wait. Finally, after "mature deliberation," the motion was tabled.[19]

Unfortunately, Van Horn totally neglected the Upper Country the next year. In a letter to her husband in 1880, Ellen White described the situation.

The poor scattered sheep [members of the Upper Country] have been left to be torn by wolves and starve without food. . . . These poor souls have had no labor and yet they seem to cling to the truth, but are starving for food. . . . He [Van Horn] is not the man for this field. He lacks promptness and energy. Adelia holds him back from his labor and he will consent to be held. They have three children. She centers all her powers on them, and labors to have him do the same and she has about succeeded.[20]

Ellen White also wrote directly to the Van Horns, but more about that as we follow their progress in the Willamette Valley.

Stephen Haskell along with Ellen and Mary White traveled to the Northwest for the region's two camp meetings in 1880. The first took place in the Upper Country at William Nichol's farm in Milton. At the gathering, delegates voted to form a new conference, the Upper Columbia Conference, from the territory east of the Cascade Mountains. This new conference started with 119 members and four churches. This left the conference west of the Cascade Mountains, the North Pacific Conference, with 102 members and five churches.[21]

George Colcord of Illinois was elected president of the Upper Columbia Conference with Alonzo Jones as his assistant. Isaac Van Horn remained in the Willamette Valley as president of the North Pacific Conference with William Raymond as an assistant.[22]

With the establishment of a permanent work force in both the Willamette Valley and the Upper Country, the General Conference hoped that the momentum of the mid-1870s would return. But this optimism for the future did not materialize. Instead, Adventism in the Northwest got bogged down with a variety of problems.

5
The Willamette Valley

The early settlers to the remote frontier of the Pacific Northwest had traveled 2,000 miles along the Oregon Trail and ended in the settler's promised land—the broad, lush Willamette Valley of western Oregon.

During the first 30 years of the Northwest's settlement, most of the travelers settled in the valley. Even after the first 30 years, the Willamette Valley and its largest city, Portland, continued to be the population, trade, and transportation center of the Northwest.

As you may remember, when Isaac Van Horn and Alonzo Jones felt that the work was well-established in Walla Walla Valley, they traveled to Willamette Valley in May 1876. They stayed with the McCords of Oregon City—a family who, in 1870, had received some tracts from a friend in Michigan and had accepted Adventism. When Van Horn and Jones arrived, they were the first Seventh-day Adventists the McCords had ever met.

From mid-May until the end of June, the two ministers held tent meetings in the state's oldest town, Oregon City. The average nightly attendance was about 100, but only one individual joined the church in this town of 1,000 inhabitants.[1]

Joseph H. Waggoner traveled by ocean steamer from California to the Northwest in late June to spend several months helping Van Horn and Jones. With this added support, Van Horn decided to direct their energies to western Oregon's second largest town—Salem.

Van Horn estimated that Salem had 6,000 inhabitants, but other sources list the population as under 2,500. The three ministers obtained permission to pitch their tent in Marion Square, a beautiful grove in the center of town where people were accustomed to public gatherings. The meetings in Salem, the state's capital, drew large crowds. Attendance averaged 350 and at times rose to 700.[2]

One of those who attended was Thomas Starbuck. His father (Elisha) had attended meetings by B. F. Snook in Iowa in the 1860s. Although Elisha had joined the Adventist church in Iowa, Thomas and the other children had not followed their father's example. In 1863, Elisha brought his family over the Oregon Trail to the Salem area. Years after Snook had preached in Iowa, he and William H. Brinkerhoff left the Adventist church and started an offshoot group called the Marion Party. Through their influence, Elisha Starbuck lost confidence in Ellen White and in church leadership.[3]

In 1868, Thomas Starbuck visited William Nichols in Windsor, California, and attended evangelistic meetings by John N. Loughborough and Daniel T. Bourdeau. Even though he did not join the Adventist church at the time, he was attracted to the message. When the *Signs of the Times* began publication in 1874, Starbuck subscribed.

His wife Almira wanted nothing to do with religion. She said she would not worship or love a God who burned the wicked forever. One day while Thomas was at work, Almira decided to read an issue of the *Signs of the Times*. An article entitled "Do the Wicked Burn Forever?" caught her attention. She read it and was amazed at what she learned.

From that time on, Almira continued secretly to read Thomas' religious magazines. As the months went by, she became convinced that she should become a Seventh-day Adventist, but she did not know how to break the news to Thomas.

At the time Van Horn opened tent meetings in Salem, Almira had a new baby, and since, in addition, she had never shown any interest in religion anyway, Thomas did not ask her if she wanted to attend the meetings with him. After Van Horn preached several sermons on the Sabbath, Thomas was convicted that he should start keeping the seventh day. One night he walked home from the meeting wondering how he would break the news to Almira. She had told him often before that she thought his father, Elisha, was crazy for observing Saturday.

Thomas knew that he had to tell his wife his decision that very evening. When he finished, Almira began crying. Through her sobs, she explained that she wished they could have taken their stand for the Sabbath together. Amazed at this turn of events, Thomas hugged his wife.[4]

In September the weather turned cold and the meetings ended. Van Horn continued working with the 30 individuals who had signed the covenant to keep the Sabbath.[5]

On January 14, 1877, Van Horn organized 11 of these individuals, eight women and three men, into the first Seventh-day Adventist Church in the Willamette Valley. Two months later, seven more individuals were baptized, including Thomas and Almira Starbuck. In May, Van Horn had another baptism which brought the membership up to 27. He also appointed Thomas as head elder of the church.[6] In later years, Thomas became successively principal of the first Adventist academy in western Oregon (North Pacific Academy), an ordained minister, and a Bible teacher at Walla Walla College.[7]

Another individual who became acquainted with Adventism at the Salem tent meetings was Obed Dickinson, a former pastor in the Congregational Church. As a young minister, he had made the long ocean voyage around the southern tip of South America in 1852 to settle in Salem when it had been only a "struggling village." Here he had built a house across the street from Marion Square and raised up a Congregational Church that became "strong and prosperous."[8]

Dickinson, a man of strong convictions, was involved in a number of reform movements. His obituary stated: "In his early pastorate of the Congregational church, when slavery was everywhere entrenched in power, and an abolitionist was an object of contempt, he was unsparing in his denunciation of the evil, so much so as at that time to interfere in a measure with his success as a pastor."[9] In 1865, Dickinson took up a new occupation. He started a seed business on a 21-acre piece of land near town. In time, his company shipped seeds to "all parts of the Pacific Coast." Dickinson became one of the most prominent men in Salem serving for many years as a trustee of Willamette University in Salem and Pacific University in Forest Grove. He also acted as director of the Salem public schools for a number of years.[10]

When Dickinson heard about Van Horn's meetings in the square across the street from his home, he decided not to attend. However, each evening he sat on his porch and listened to the messages. As the meetings progressed, Dickinson found that he could not prove Van Horn wrong. Secretly he searched through his seminary textbooks but found no opposing answers. He wrote to his professors in Boston, but their responses proved unacceptable to him.

For two years Dickinson secretly observed the Sabbath and searched for answers. However, his study drew him closer and closer to the Adventists. In 1878, he told his wife that he was joining the Seventh-day Adventist Church. She became furious! She enjoyed the prestige of belonging to the popular Congregational Church. In spite of opposition from his wife and daughter, Dickinson stood firm. From that time on, Mrs. Dickinson refused to let her husband bring Adventist literature into their home. So Obed Dickinson was forced to read his Adventist publications in the garden office. His wife maintained her opposition to him and his new religion for as long as he lived.[11]

After the treasurer of the young North Pacific Conference, William Leavitt, stole a third of the conference's annual income in 1881, Dickinson took over the job. He continued conscientiously to serve in this position until his death in 1892.[12] At the 1891 General Conference session, District Six superintendent R. A. Underwood stated that the strong financial standing of the North Pacific Conference was due largely "to the faithful labors of Father Dickinson."[13]

Alonzo Jones held his first series of evangelistic meetings in September 1876 in Eola, a small village near Salem. He organized a church of eight members. Next, he conducted meetings in the Oak Grove schoolhouse and in Jefferson.[14] Van Horn concentrated his efforts in Salem during the winter months. By May he reported:

> The church [Salem] hold their meetings in a meetinghouse near the center of the city, owned by the South Methodist church. They pay $5 per month rent, which is reasonable. . . . I see no reason now why the cause in Salem may not prosper. . . . Had we left Salem last fall I don't think we should have seen anywhere near so good a result.[15]

In early 1877, James White wrote Van Horn suggesting that he take John N. Loughborough's place as president of the California Conference. Van Horn was opposed to the idea, saying that California needed "a wiser head than mine."[16]

When Waggoner visited the Northwest in the summer of 1876, he had with him a surprise for Adelia Van Horn—her sister, Frances E.

Patten. Originally, Frances was planning to leave the Northwest with Waggoner at the end of the tent season but decided to stay longer. Undoubtedly, her attraction to Van Horn's young assistant, Alonzo Jones, was a motivating factor in the decision. For in April 1877, Alonzo and Frances were married. The newlyweds moved in with the Van Horns.[17] In his biography of Jones, George Knight points out that in time "domestic difficulties" brought that living arrangement to an end.[18] Van Horn claimed that in the late 1870s these problems caused Jones to withdraw from him and "labored afterward mostly by himself."[19]

Part of the difficulties between the two families could have stemmed from Frances' poor health. In a letter to James White, Adelia described the situation.

> She [Frances] has been sick much of the time since she has been here, and of course has not been that help that she otherwise might have been. She has been afflicted . . . with something like 'St. Anthony's fire,' causing considerable suffering at times. . . . She has had three attacks of diphtheria since the Typhoid fever last winter. And for two days past we have been working to save her from pneumonia.[20]

Jones planned to return East during the summer of 1877 to visit the aging grandparents who had raised him and to attend Battle Creek College in Michigan. Since Jones' grandparents in Ohio were "worth considerable property," he felt "it would be for his financial interest to go there."[21] When James White, president of the General Conference, learned of these plans, he sent a letter to the young preacher reminding him that there was a shortage of ministers in the Northwest and suggesting that he stay put.[22]

Portland began emerging as the trade and transportation center for the Northwestern frontier as early as the 1850s. Its ideal location near the Columbia River which served as a highway for ocean-bound ships and inland-bound steamboats and at the northernmost end of the Willamette Valley made it a natural center of population. Throughout the frontier period of the Northwest, Portland continued as the transportation hub between the largest city of the West Coast—San Francisco—and the various regions of the Pacific Northwest.[23]

After conducting tent meetings in Dallas, Van Horn and Jones turned their efforts in July 1877 toward Portland with its nearly 15,000 inhabitants. They conducted meetings in their 60-foot tent at Eighth and Yamhill. Later they changed to a location on the east side of the Willamette River, but met with only limited success.[24]

The same year that Van Horn and Jones held their effort in Portland, R. D. Benham, who had been a soldier in the Civil War and a prisoner in a Confederate prison camp, moved from Iowa to Beaverton, an area southwest of Portland. Benham began sharing his faith and soon a group of 18 accepted the Adventist message and began meeting in the Benham's home for services. In 1878, this group was organized and became the third Adventist church in the Willamette Valley. Several years later the Beaverton Church erected the first Adventist church structure in western Oregon. Benham attended Healdsburg College, now Pacific Union College, in California in 1884-85 and returned to western Oregon where he served as a minister for about 25 years.[25]

Van Horn and Jones planned the first camp meeting for the Northwest in Salem during 1878 . John Loughborough and Ellen White attended the gathering. William Raymond was ordained to the ministry at the closing service.[26]

Raymond had joined the Salem Church in 1876, but he never fully had embraced Adventism. Some eight years later Van Horn wrote: "Brother Raymond was crooked on points of doctrine and some of the prophecies when he came among us. I had many talks with him which seemingly had little effect. He is much inclined to his own way." In spite of these theological problems, however, Van Horn and Loughborough rushed him into the ministry. This proved to be a mistake which caused a major problem to Northwestern Adventism in the mid-1880s.[27]

Several months after the camp meeting, Ellen White wrote to the Van Horns telling them she had been shown how they had neglected the conference work, especially evangelism, stewardship education, and administration. She urged them to give God their best efforts in the future.[28] The Van Horns asked the General Conference leaders to transfer them from the Northwest in 1878 and 1879. The busy leaders ignored their requests.[29]

The Van Horns during this time didn't put into practice the counsel that Ellen White had given them. She was very disappointed at what she found when she visited the 1880 camp meeting in Milton, Oregon. It was after this camp meeting that in a letter to her husband, White pointed out that Van Horn had spent most of the past year building a house for his family in Beaverton, while he neglected his evangelistic and pastoral work in the Willamette Valley and totally ignored the believers in the Upper Country.[30]

Four days later Ellen wrote another letter to her husband, stating: He [Van Horn] is not the man for this field. . . . Adelia holds him back from his labors; and he will consent to be held. . . . I felt the time had come to make direct appeals to the ministers [Van Horn and Jones]. . . . I then bore to them a most pointed testimony. . . . I think Elder Van Horn begins to see something of his true condition, and as he is naturally a conscientious man I think he will not rest until there is a reformation in himself.[31]

With these views in mind Ellen wrote her testimony to the Van Horns. Van Horn wrote to Ellen White in August 1880 saying that he accepted the testimony that she had given him.[32]

After the 1878 camp meeting, Van Horn and Jones rarely worked together. Jones went to conduct meetings in Eugene City (now Eugene) and organized a small church of 14 members. Then he held meetings in Damascus, organizing a church of 11 members.[33] Meanwhile Van Horn worked in the Upper Country and in Salem.[34]

We have no record of Jones and Raymond's activities during late 1879 and early 1880, because none of the three Northwestern ministers sent any reports to the *Review and Herald*.[35]

The tension between Van Horn and Jones intensified by 1880. In a letter to Ellen White, Van Horn stated: "I hear nothing from Brother Jones. I have written to him but get no reply. I hope and most earnestly pray he may not make shipwreck of his faith in the message."[36]

When the territory of the Northwest was divided into two conferences at the Milton camp meetings in 1880. the action made it even more possible for Van Horn and Jones to go their separate ways.

After the Milton camp meeting, Van Horn traveled with Raymond to Forest Grove in the Willamette Valley. There they held a series of meetings that met with few results.[37]

The Van Horns were transferred the next summer to California. Shortly after, they returned to the East where Van Horn divided his time between traveling to the various camp meetings with General Conference president George Butler and working with the churches in Michigan.[38]

M. Ellsworth Olsen in A *History of the Origin and Progress of Seventh-day Adventism* mentions that while on the camp meeting circuit Van Horn was "often asked to conduct meetings for the children, and his tender, heart-to-heart talks on such practical subjects as conversion, repentance, and obedience to God's law are gratefully remembered by not a few men and women of today."[39] Van Horn was president of the Michigan Conference from 1889-1893. Then he was asked to be superintendent of the General Conference district number one (eastern Canada and the Atlantic Coast states). From 1898 to 1903 he worked in Indiana and in Battle Creek, Michigan. He died in 1910.[40]

Perhaps because of his close association with George Butler (in the late 1880s) and the tension that existed between him and his brother-in-law, Alonzo Jones, Van Horn rejected the message of righteousness by faith at the 1888 General Conference session. Ellen White wrote to him about this.[41] In his reply, Van Horn stated,

> This communication by your hand to me I heartily accept as a testimony from the Lord. It reveals to me the sad condition I have been in since the Minneapolis meeting, and this reproof from the Lord is just and true. . . . If you have anything further that would give me more light, showing me more clearly my true condition, I shall be very glad to receive it.[42]

Arthur Spalding, in his book *Captains of the Host*, said that "I. D. Van Horn was one of the best beloved ministers through the last half of the century. He had the gift of the common touch."[43]

When Van Horn left the Willamette Valley in 1881, the North Pacific Conference with nearly 120 members was still struggling, the region's largest city still had no Adventist church, the five congregations were small and without buildings, and most of the conference territory, including the Puget Sound area of western Washington Territory, was still unentered.

Perhaps the shift in his efforts to caring for family problems to the neglect of his ministerial responsibilities brought on a general decline in the work of the conference and discouragement to the members.

6
Ellen White Visits the Northwestern Frontier

The young Seventh-day Adventist Church specialized in attracting crowds through tent evangelism. The ministers traveled from town to town erecting canvas meeting houses and presenting lectures. Many people in these communities attended the meetings out of curiosity; usually a few joined the church. The tent-meeting approach proved to be the most successful method of presenting the Gospel in unworked towns. However, though tent evangelism worked well, the foremost crowd-getter became the annual Adventist camp meetings. It was not uncommon for a small conference of several hundred members to attract an audience of several thousand at the camp meeting.

The church leaders soon realized that with such large crowds they needed to feature their best preachers. Camp meetings were scheduled to follow one another so that each conference could count on top-notch speakers. One of the denomination's most sought-after speakers was Ellen White. Non-Adventist audiences especially enjoyed her presentations on temperance. During the 1870s, Ellen and James White averaged seven camp meetings each season. In 1876, Ellen did the seemingly impossible feat of attending 14 different camp meetings.[1] During the frontier days of the 1870s and early 1880s, Ellen White made three visits to the camp meetings of the Pacific Northwest. James was unable to accompany her on the first two trips due to his poor health. By the third trip, he had died.

Isaac Van Horn planned the first camp meeting in the Pacific Northwest in a grove of tall fir trees on Adam Stephen's farm about three miles north of Salem. The chosen site bordered on the Oregon &

California Railroad that served the north and central portions of western Oregon. When Van Horn visited the railroad officials, they promised that all regular trains would stop at the campgrounds during the event and that camp meeting attendees who paid full fare to the campground would receive a free trip home.[2]

However, railroad service between California and the Pacific Northwest was not yet in existence. The key speakers for the event, Ellen White and John Loughborough, had to travel to the area by steamer, boarding at San Francisco. After three days of rough ocean travel their steamer sailed into the wide, peaceful Columbia River and followed it to Portland.[3]

Describing her first ocean voyage in a *Signs of the Times* article, Ellen wrote:

> I had been overworked, and was much worn, and flattered myself that I should rest on board the steamer. But the wind blew very strong directly against us, I remained on deck after nearly all had abandoned it because of sea-sickness, I enjoyed the sight of the billows running mountain high, blue and green . . . I remained on deck until dark, and then went into the cabin, where the pitching of the boat made me very sick. This was Monday and I was unable to sit up from that time until Thursday morning.

Most of the passengers experienced severe seasickness on the first three days of the trip. On Thursday, the steamer entered the calm waters of the Columbia River and the seasick passengers recovered and started walking around on deck.

On the evening of the fourth day, as Ellen was resting in her stateroom with her door partially open, she overheard a conversation by Elder Brown, a minister from another denomination. He was talking about her with a small group. He stated, "Mrs. White is all law, law; she believes that we must be saved by the law, and no one can be saved unless they keep the law."

The injustice of being thus misrepresented stirred Ellen. She emerged from her stateroom and responded:

> That is a false statement. Mrs. White has never occupied that

position. I will speak for myself and for our people. We have always taken the position that there is no power in the law to save a single transgressor of the law. . . . Elder Brown, please never again make the misstatement that we do not rely on Jesus Christ for salvation, but trust in the law to be saved.

Ellen took this opportunity to straighten out the group on her position concerning the subject of the law and salvation. When she finished, Elder Brown claimed that that was not what Adventists taught in California. At that, Ellen invited the group to the upcoming camp meeting in Salem. She told them that they could find out for themselves what she taught at that gathering.

Though Ellen appreciated the kind attention provided by Captain Conner and his assistants, she was happy when they reached Portland.[4] She was ready for solid ground again. She wrote, "When I got off the boat . . . it seemed to me as though I was still on the boat, and I would step so high that people must have thought I was drunk."[5]

Ellen was thrilled to see Isaac and Adelia Van Horn whom she claimed as her own children. She was impressed with the Van Horns' work as missionaries in the Northwest. She wrote:

Brother Van Horn, with characteristic modesty, has not furnished as full and favorable reports of his work as he might justly have done. I was accordingly somewhat surprised, and very much pleased to find the cause of God in so prosperous a condition in Oregon.[6]

When Ellen reached Salem, via train, she accepted a number of speaking appointments. One evening she gave a discourse in the Methodist church, the largest church structure in Oregon and the entire Northwest, on her favorite subject—temperance. On another occasion, she spoke to 150 men at the State prison.[7] Ellen described her visit to the prison.

At a signal from a bell, two men opened the great iron gates by means of a lever. . . . The doors were securely closed . . . for the first time in my life, I was immured in prison walls. I had anticipated seeing a set of repulsive looking men. In this I was disappointed; many of them seemed to be intelligent, and some appeared to be men of ability.

As the men "heartily" sang the hymns, Ellen began thinking about how their mothers must feel. This influenced her talk. In a letter to her husband, she wrote: "I tried to imagine the youth around me as my boys, and to talk with them from a mother's heart of love and sympathy."[8]

Ellen received several visions during the six-day camp meeting. One short vision concerning her husband came to her as she spoke on Friday morning. She wrote:

I tried to speak, but my utterance was broken because of weeping. I had felt very anxious about my husband on account of his poor health. While speaking, a meeting in the church in Battle Creek came vividly before my mind's eye, my husband being in the midst, with the mellow light of the Lord resting upon and surrounding him. His face bore the marks of health, and he was apparently very happy. . . . I can never represent to others the picture that vividly impressed my mind on that occasion. For a moment the extent of the work came before me, and I lost sight of my surroundings. The occasion and the people I was addressing passed from my mind. The light, the precious light from heaven, was shining in great brilliancy upon those institutions which are engaged in the solemn and elevated work of reflecting the rays of light that heaven has let shine upon them.

In *Testimonies for the Church*, vol. 4, Ellen also commented on the other visions:

All through this camp meeting the Lord seemed very near me. When it closed, I was exceedingly weary, but free in the Lord. . . . Just before the camp meeting commenced, in the night season, many things were opened to me in vision; but silence was enjoined upon me that I should not mention the matter to anyone at that time. After the meeting closed, I had in the night season another remarkable manifestation of God's power.[9]

The members of the small North Pacific Conference were pleased with the results of their first camp meeting. When the visitors from

Salem were urged to attend on Sunday, "It was estimated that two thousand people were on the ground[s]." On the final day of the gathering, the believers enjoyed a wonderful time together where hearts were softened. It was at that meeting that William Raymond was ordained to the ministry.[10]

Camp meetings in the 1870s in many parts of the Wild West had developed a bad reputation for being rough, disorderly gatherings. Van Horn was pleased when both the Portland and Salem newspapers mentioned that the Adventists maintained "good order." One wealthy farmer of the area stated to his friends that "he never saw a camp meeting before that he would take his wife and daughters to, but now he was going right home and bring them to this meeting."

At the camp meeting in Walla Walla the following year, the public also was impressed with the way Adventists conducted their annual gatherings. James F. Wood wrote: "The ground was thronged with strangers. . . . The general exclamation was, 'I never saw such a camp meeting as this—so quiet, such order.'"[11]

On the Sunday following the western Oregon camp meeting, Ellen White traveled into Salem and addressed a crowd of 250 in the public square. Her topic was "The Simplicity of Gospel Religion."[12] Three days later Ellen headed home aboard the steamer *Idaho* with hopes of a better voyage. Edith Donaldson, the daughter of an Adventist family in Salem, joined her for the trip. Ellen promised Edith's parents that she would accompany their daughter to Battle Creek College.

The captain of the steamer told Ellen that she could keep her porthole open, but soon after she had opened the little window the two women heard a terrible sound. Ellen wrote later that she turned to look and "a stream of water rushed into my berth." Even though the steward soon had everything cleaned up, Ellen lost one commodity that she greatly valued—fresh air.[13]

The dining saloon had a special table for the wealthy men of Oakland and San Francisco. One man in his sixties became especially drunk. Ellen wrote: "He held it [wine] up so that all at the table could view it. 'Here,' said he, 'is my Christ, all the Christ I want, gentlemen. This is my Jesus. This is good cheer,' and drained the glass, others following his example."[14]

Two years later Ellen boarded another steamer for her second ocean voyage to Portland. This time she was accompanied by Willie White's wife Mary and S. N. Haskell. At Portland, they transferred to a steamboat for the trip up the Columbia River.[15]

Two camp meetings were planned for the Pacific Northwest in 1880. The first was to take place on the east side of the Cascade Mountains on William Nichols' farm in Milton, Oregon.[16] Ellen, arriving in Walla Walla about a week and a half before the camp meeting was to start, stayed with the Wood family who lived about three miles from town. She referred to them as kind, hospitable people. Ellen traveled with them to town several times and spoke to the members at the church.[17]

In a testimony to the Walla Walla church, Ellen pointed out that they had "greatly backslidden from God." She laid much of the blame on a Brother C. (The E. G. White Estate never has been able to identify this brother.) She wrote: "He has been picking flaws in others, living on their mistakes; and this is spiritual starvation. Every revival is liable to bring persons into the church who are not really converted. They hold the truth nominally, but are not sanctified by its sweet influence."[18]

Ellen also was quite distressed about Van Horn's neglect of the work east of the Cascade Mountains. Her heart went out to the "poor sheep and lambs" who were "perish[ing] without food." On May 20, Ellen traveled to the campgrounds at Milton where 40 tents and a number of covered wagons were prepared. On Friday afternoon she spoke to the people. She wrote her husband:

> I spoke in the afternoon with great freedom in a very pointed manner, but the darkness seemed so great. There has been great prejudice against me which I had not known, but I am not troubled about this. God can remove it away.

At the Milton gathering, Ellen confronted a number of individuals about their problems. The testimonies presented at both the Milton and Salem camp meetings have been published in *Testimonies for the Church*, vol. 5, pp. 249-289 and 298-309.

Ellen was especially concerned about Isaac Van Horn. She told her husband that he "preached a wordy, fluent discourse, but without point, generalizing everything but hitting nothing." On May 23, Ellen called Van Horn and Alonzo Jones into her tent. She "bore to them a most pointed testimony and charged the state of the churches upon the course Elder Van Horn had pursued in doing nothing. . . . It was a weeping, and confessing time. There was a humbling of soul before God."[19]

Ellen also tackled the sensitive problem of some who had reneged on their pledges. When John N. Loughborough had organized the North Pacific Mission as a conference in 1877, the members of the newly formed conference had enthusiastically pledged to support the Pacific Press by purchasing $5,000 worth of stock. Each member of the auditing committee had made large pledges to help the group reach its goal.[20] Soon after the meeting, several of the Milton church members changed their minds concerning the pledges, and as a result did not pay them. In a testimony to Brother A (William Nichols from Milton), Ellen stated: "He thought how much he could do with his means by investing it in worldly enterprises."[21] In a sermon at the 1891 Michigan camp meeting, Ellen explained how she addressed this problem.

There were all these men of wealth. Those who had the most were complaining the most. Here they were with all their complaints, when I stepped into the desk and asked what they were complaining about. I knew what they were complaining about, and said to Brother Miller [Aaron Miller from Milton], "You invested so much money in the cause. What did you do after you pledged this much? You went and talked your disaffection, and God cut your crops down according to your withholding. . . . We want to elevate this conference," said I, and turned around to Brother Van Horn, and told him to put my name down in place of Brother Miller's. "I will stand where he stands. I will be responsible for him." I called for another in the same way, and when I called for a third, they got ashamed and began to feel that they would not allow Sister White to pay their money.

"Now," said I, "Elder Van Horn told me how much money was paid by the General Conference to put the truth into Oregon. Now tell me how much money Oregon has paid to the General Conference?" It fell short something near $1,000 of what the General Conference had purely invested for them to bring the truth to them. That was a showing they had not looked at. They were ashamed of this. The light of heaven has not shone upon some of them since that time.[22]

One "white-headed man" had traveled 140 miles by horseback and on foot to attend the meetings. It was the first Adventist sermon he had heard in six years.[23]

On Sundays, a large non-Adventist crowd of between 800 and 1,000 gathered at the campgrounds. One of them, a Dunkard preacher from Pataha Prairie (near present-day Pomeroy), attended all of the meetings. At the end of the camp meeting, he begged Ellen to visit his church. If the church had not been "seventy-five miles by private conveyance over a rough road," she would have gone.[24]

After the Milton camp meeting, the California delegation took the steamboat back to Portland. Here Ellen spoke to a small group of Adventists in Beaverton and Portland, the temperance society, and the members of the Methodist church. The camp meeting for the Willamette Valley believers was held at Marion Square in the heart of Salem. About 25 tents dotted the grounds and 150 members attended the gathering. Ellen stayed in the John Donaldson family home.

Although the camp meeting location was not as quiet or conducive for meditation as a rural setting, it proved to be a perfect site for the general public. Haskell reported:

> On Sunday the tent was crowded, both day and evening, by attentive audiences; while in the afternoon there was the most intense interest manifest to hear sister White, who spoke for two hours on the subject of Christian temperance.[25]

On Sabbath, Ellen met with the Adventist believers in a special meeting. In a letter to her husband she stated: "[I] bore to them testimonies given me of God for individual cases. This was an important meeting, and many confessions were made."[26] Mrs. Sherwood of the Salem Church received one of the testimonies. At one point during the meeting, Ellen pointed her finger at the woman and said, "You have kept scores of honest people out of this church."[27]

At the strong urging of the leaders of the Methodist church, Ellen stayed an additional week in Salem. She spoke three times in their "grand building" to crowds of around 700 people on the subject of temperance. One of the Methodist ministers told an Adventist member that "he regretted Mrs. White was not a staunch Methodist, for they would make her a bishop at once; she could do justice to the office."[28]

Summarizing to Edson and Emma White her seven-week trip to the Pacific Northwest, Ellen wrote:

> It is impossible for me to describe the burden which I have borne upon my soul in Oregon and Washington Territory. I have spoken already about twenty-six times on this coast, and have written a great number of pages.[29]

7
William Nichols

During the early 1800s the nation's frontier continued to advance westward across the continent.

To reach the West Coast, settlers trudged across a vast and desolate wilderness. The undeveloped route they followed to the Willamette Valley in western Oregon was known as the Oregon Trail because it resembled a trail more than a road.

For most travelers, the trip across the 2,000-mile Oregon Trail was a nightmare they were happy to put behind them. The trip was extremely dangerous; in fact, one estimate is that roughly one in every ten travelers, about 30,000, died on their journey west. Disease, especially cholera, was the primary killer; but thousands died of Indian attacks, accidents, and drownings at river crossings. It was not uncommon for the travelers to be accidentally shot, run over by a wagon, or caught in a buffalo stampede.[1]

One traveler, William Babcock, made his trip in 1859. His diary account of the trip reveals some of the hardships these pioneers faced:

> I could not find any water so I had to go without all day. I think I never suffered so much in my life. . . . Our wagons were frequently stuck in the mud. . . . Forded a very bad river. Two wagons were capsized. . . . The mosquitoes are so bad as to be almost unendurable. . . . The road was so dusty that a person could hardly breathe. . . . One of my oxen got sick and laid down and died. . . . Saw the first house [eastern Oregon] since leaving the Platte River [1,500 miles]. Some of the men seemed almost crazy, they whooped and hallowed and acted like wild men.[2]

Why did Seventh-day Adventists risk the dangers and hardships of this trip to come to the Wild West? What motivated them to make the trip? The primary force drawing these hardy Adventists westward seems to have been the lure of prime farm land. They were willing to endure the rigors and dangers so they could build a better future for their families. Others, like William Nichols, came West either to avoid the Civil War or to find adventure.

Nichols, who was born near Montreal, was converted at the age of six while listening to a series of William Miller's meetings. Twelve years later, in 1856, he moved to Iowa where he learned of Adventism and joined the newly established Adventist church in La Porte City.

In 1862, Nichols traveled West along with many gold seekers who were heading to the recently discovered gold fields in the Elkhorn Mountains of eastern Oregon.[3] On their way they encountered the Shoshone and Bannock Indians of the Snake River region. They proved to be especially hostile, frequently attacking the wagon trains. Most diary accounts of the trip of 1862 comment on the problems encountered with the Indians along the Snake River in what is today southern Idaho. Sarah Howard wrote in her diary that they found some survivors of a massacre nearby "the road turning off to California. . . . Our Captain was shot by Indians about the same time, but eventually recovered." Evan McComas wrote that when his wagon train arrived at the Raft River it "seems to be one continual battleground." And Jane Gould wrote that her wagon train was also attacked by the Indians. After coming on the remains of the massacre at what is today called Massacre Rock, she wrote: "I wish all Indians in Christendom were exterminated."[4] A similar experience beset William Nichols.

After crossing the Raft River, his wagon train was ambushed by Indians. He wrote:

> Every night [between the Raft and Burnt Rivers] . . . [we] witnessed the repulsion of Indian attacks, and several days the murder of [our] companions or the finding of dead white men that had been waylaid and scalped by those desert Arabs.[5]

When finally reaching the Northwest, Nichols spent his first year in the Rogue River Valley of southern Oregon. There, he and a group of 50 citizens helped Colonel C. S. Drew and his soldiers establish Fort Klamath to provide protection for the settlers of this new frontier. He spent the next year in the Willamette Valley. Then Nichols boarded a ship to New York. In San Francisco his plans changed when he became violently sick with the "fever." While recuperating, he visited the Spence family in the Russian River Valley, friends with whom he had crossed the plains two years earlier. A year later, Nichols married Sarah Spence and they settled on a farm.[6]

When Nichols first arrived in the Russian River Valley, only a few Seventh-day Adventists were scattered throughout the entire western frontier. In 1864, he wrote in a letter to the *Review and Herald*:

I feel that if there ever was a state [California] that needed to be enlightened in regard to the Advent doctrine and Sabbath, it is this one. The other day I heard of a Seventh-day Adventist, and started to hunt him up. I inquired of a man if he knew of any one that kept the seventh day for the Sabbath. Oh, says he, that kind of folks are all dead long ago; the last was an old man in Ohio who died ten years ago. I told him he was mistaken; for there were some left yet. I found the man I was looking for; but he was a first-day Adventist [Advent Christian].[7]

After holding a successful series of tent meetings in 1868 in Petaluma, California, John N. Loughborough and Daniel T. Bourdeau accepted Nichols and Thomas Starbuck's invitation to hold meetings in Windsor in the Russian River Valley.[8] Nichols invited his friends and neighbors to the meetings. Several of these individuals, Aaron Miller and James F. Wood among them, joined the church. Wood became so excited about Adventism that he moved back to the Walla Walla Valley. He also encouraged Nichols and Miller to settle in the Northwest with him, which they did in 1871.[9]

Nichols became a wealthy man. The average Northwestern farmer of 1885 owned property worth about $1,000, but Nichols' holdings were valued at $6,100.[10] He owned 400 acres in the Milton area and bought 300 acres in Washington Territory about 16 miles southwest of Spokane at Medical Lake, whose waters supposedly contained medicinal properties. A history of Spokane County written in 1900 notes:

It has been designated as the "modern pool of Bethesda" because of the surprising cures which it has effected. . . . From time unknown we are told the curative properties were known to the Indians who congregated in great numbers around its shores, bringing the afflicted from all directions.

Nichols and other businessmen capitalized on the lake's reputation and erected motels, marketed the lake water, and sold the medical salt produced by evaporation.[11] Nichols' friend Aaron Miller also became a wealthy man. He started the first plant nursery in the Walla Walla Valley. His business, Milton Nursery, eventually hired 100 seasonal and 50 year-round workers, shipping products to all parts of the United States. (One of Miller's great-great grandsons, Robert S. Folkenberg, is currently [1996] president of the eight-million-member, global Seventh-day Adventist Church.[12]

Aaron Miller and his brother Joshua crossed the plains in 1849 to search for gold in California. Ten years later he moved to Missouri where he married Samaria Bradfield. In 1863 Miller and his family returned to California by covered wagon where he took up farming. On this trip across the California Trail, he served as the captain of their small caravan of five wagons.[13]

When the Millers and Nichols moved to the Milton area, Aaron Miller erected a log house for his family. In a newspaper interview, Samaria Miller described what life had been like in the early days: "Neighbors were not close and Mrs. Miller says she used to stand by the window of her home and cry because she was so lonely. Indians were frequent callers and helped themselves to many things."[14]

When a Seventh-day Adventist church was established in Milton in 1876, Nichols and Miller moved their memberships from the Walla Walla church. Both men remained members of the Milton church until their deaths in the 1920s and 30s.[15]

At some point in his early experience with Adventism, Nichols became involved with the Iowa dissidents of the Marion Party who opposed church leadership and Ellen White. He still held some of these unsupportive attitudes in the 1880s and was influencing others in the Milton church.

Nichols' domineering personality and independent-minded

attitudes caused him to clash with each of the leaders that the General Conference sent to the Upper Columbia Conference. Ellen White wrote a description of how Nichols and the Milton church treated the conference's first president, George Colcord:

> The Milton Church ran things and did not magnify his [Colcord's] office. They would criticize his preaching and dictate to him until he was manipulated like a ball of putty. He was president only in name, and lost his courage. . . . Brother Nichols would order the ministers as though he knew all about the work.[16]

This problem and a number of others brought on a major crisis for the Adventist Church in the Northwest.

After Sarah Nichols died, William began corresponding with Ada Colcord, the widow of George Colcord, whom he had harassed in the 1880s. They were married in 1906.[17]

Under strong leadership from William Nichols, the Milton church established the Milton Academy in 1886. At its peak four years later the academy enrolled 150 students. That same year, Adventists in the Northwest decided to close their two academies and start a college. When the committee selected Walla Walla instead of Milton as the site for the new college, Nichols and the Milton church became so angry they refused to cooperate with the college project.[18] More about this in a later chapter.

Later, they did reconsider and began supporting the new school—Walla Walla College. In fact, George Nichols, William's son, moved to College Place and became the business manager of the college in 1893, continuing in this position until 1902.[19]

The Upper Columbia Conference erected a building in 1892 on College Avenue; today it is known as the College Store. From this building, Clarence and Minnie Ford operated a Tract and Missionary Society store for many years. In May 1897, William Nichols and his son Dorsey purchased this building and opened William Nichols & Son General Merchandise. For ten years, Dorsey operated this dry goods and grocery store as well as the College Place Post Office.[20]

From fighting Indians along the Oregon Trail to fighting conference presidents in the Walla Walla Valley, William Nichols' life was never dull. He may have been domineering and, at times, fanatical, but he also was highly committed to the message of Adventism and the goals of Christian education. In many ways, William Nichols' strong, determined style was typical of the men and women who settled the western frontier. They may not have been as loving and polished as their descendants, but then, they were living in the Wild West.

8

New Leaders for the Northwest

With the formation of the Upper Columbia Conference in 1880 and the departure of Isaac Van Horn in 1881, a new set of leaders was sent to the frontier of the Pacific Northwest. George Colcord was assigned by the General Conference leaders to the Upper Country in 1880, and the delegates to the first session of the Upper Columbia Conference elected him as their president.

Colcord had been introduced to Adventism in 1855 while teaching school in Illinois. Several years later, he entered the ministry and was attending Battle Creek College in Michigan when he was called to serve in the Northwest.[1] The Colcords arrived in Milton in time for camp meeting, so George assisted the other ministers with the preaching. In a report in the *Review and Herald*, Stephen Haskell notes that Colcord's "preaching was appreciated by all present, and both he and his wife seemed to win their way to the hearts of the people."[2]

We have no record of the early activities of Colcord but we do know that he was named president of the new Upper Columbia Conference and Alonzo Jones was appointed his assistant. Early in 1882, Jones held a successful series of meetings in Farmington in Washington Territory. The meetings were canceled after a month because of a smallpox epidemic, but Jones was able to organize a church. During the next two years, he spent much of his time with this group and erected a 20- x 30-foot church building for them.[3]

One of Jones's converts in Farmington was Will W. Steward, a young man who soon attended Healdsburg College in California. Following college, Steward served for many years as a minister in the

Upper Columbia Conference and became the first president of the Idaho Conference.[4]

Jones wrote both Willie and Ellen White in 1883 urging them to visit Farmington. He wrote, "If you shall come the whole community with one accord will turn out to hear you." He also asked Willie to help him purchase a bell for the new Farmington church. The community had raised the money for both the bell and belfry.[5]

The Upper Columbia Conference camp meeting of 1882 was held in Dayton in Washington Territory. Joseph H. Waggoner of California attended the gathering and reported in the *Signs of the Times* that

> . . . immigrants are literally pouring into eastern Washington [Territory] and Oregon induced to come by the opening up of the country by the building of railroads. . . . The moving mania seems to seize all classes, and our churches are seriously affected by it. . . . The inducement to take up land has been quite strong, but Brother Colcord has resisted it, and given his whole being to the work of the message.

Waggoner also noted that the "moving mania" especially was affecting the Walla Walla church. He stated: "Most of the brethren have gone away, so that there are few male members left. It has been feared that the house (church building) would become useless, if the moving spirit continued to prevail."[6]

A serious problem arose in 1880 that hampered the work in the Upper Columbia Conference. William Nichols and the members of the Milton church criticized Colcord's preaching and dictated to him "until he was manipulated like a ball of putty." Their harsh treatment discouraged him and eventually "everything in the conference ran down."[7] The stress caused by these insensitive members undermined Colcord's health. At the 1882 camp meeting, he was "taken with a severe chill" which "prostrated him" so he was "not able to preach during all the [camp] meeting."[8] Six months later he still reported poor health.[9]

Colcord and Jones continued to hold evangelistic meetings in the small towns of the Upper Country, and by 1883 four Adventist groups were meeting in eastern Oregon—Alba, Basket Mountain, Echo, and

Milton—and four in Washington Territory—Dayton, Farmington, Pataha, and Walla Walla.[10]

In 1883, Clarence Ford, who had married the Woods' daughter, Minnie, was given a ministerial license and began working as Colcord's tent master. Their first series of meetings was held in Goldendale in Washington Territory. Even though they met with strong opposition, they were able to organize a church of nine members.[11]

Alonzo Jones spent so much time in Farmington in 1882 and 1883 that Willie White wrote him early in 1884 asking why. In April, Jones replied.

> Our people here [Farmington] are all poor . . . [and] as there was barely enough money available to buy material [for a church building], of course, there was none with which to hire carpenters to build it. So I went to work and built it with my own hands. . . . Besides that, the membership of the church has been doubled [from 13 to 26]. . . . Well, when the church was built and dedicated, I was in debt some on the building. . . . Then the directors of the school district came to me with the unanimous request that I should teach school. This opened the way for me to pay off my debts without taxing the Conference for anything. . . . So this is what I have been doing. . . . All this may not meet your approval . . . And where, in any point I have done wrong, I ask pardon.

At the end of his letter, Jones asked White for a favor.

> Now, my dear brother, I want to tell you something on my own account. Here it is—I WANT TO GO EAST. I want to go to learn. I want to go to school. I want to see the workings of the Cause there. And I want to learn how to do rightly what may fall to my lot. . . . I hardly suppose you will have any objections. Sister White told me the last time she was here, to go as soon as I could. . . . So now, PLEASE LET ME GO.[12]

After the 1884 camp meeting in Walla Walla, Jones was finally rewarded for his years of service in the northwestern frontier by being transferred to California, the center of Adventism on the West Coast. Here his popularity mushroomed. In four short years he went from being an unknown minister in the Wild West to the spiritual hero of Adventism—a man who brought "a most precious message" to God's people.

In the late 1880s and 1890s, Jones returned to the Northwest, speaking at the camp meetings in both Northwestern conferences. It was reported that for the first graduation of Walla Walla College he spoke two hours and twenty minutes.[13]

During the summer of 1884, George Colcord and Clarence Ford held tent meetings in Colfax and Garfield in Washington Territory with little results.[14] Loughborough, who was serving as the interim president of the Upper Columbia Conference, visited the group in Colfax. He wrote:

> After a sixty-five-mile ride on a stage over the dustiest road I ever saw in my life [from Dayton], I came to Colfax. . . . The church members [other denominations] for the most part banded themselves to stay away from the meetings, and the rest of the town are mostly for this world. A very few are taking their stand for truth.[15]

In early 1885, the Colcords moved to Nevada where George hoped to regain his health.[16] Before leaving the Northwest, he wrote a hymn that reflects to some extent his experience in the Upper Country. It was published in the *Signs of the Times*. The words to the first stanza are:

> Almost home! O words so cheering,
> To all Christians pilgrims here!
> Now their journey's end is nearing;
> Soon they'll reach their home so dear.
> Self-denial, burdens, crosses,
> Pain and tears have been their lot.
> Soon in paradise, their losses,
> Everyone will be forgot.
> Almost home! Proclaiming by singing:
> Sing, ye saints, with ardent soul;
> Rouse the careless; With voice and ringing,

Shout: We soon shall reach the goal![17]

In 1882, Charles L. Boyd moved to western Oregon to take the presidency of the North Pacific Conference with its five churches and 123 members.[18] From 1872-1878, Boyd and Robert M. Kilgore pioneered the Adventist work in Nebraska. In September 1878, Boyd had been elected as the president of the newly formed Nebraska Conference with its 17 churches and 350 members. He continued to serve in this position until his transfer to the Northwest.[19]

Boyd, a widower, had married Maud Sisley two years earlier. She had just returned from Southampton, England, where she had been assisting John Loughborough as a Bible instructor and literature evangelist. She also had served in Switzerland as the denomination's first woman missionary in a foreign country. Here she had assisted John N. Andrews with his publishing work.[20]

In the summer of 1882, the Boyds arrived in the Northwest and attended the camp meeting in Salem. Since the North Pacific Conference had been without a president for a year, the members were discouraged and the work was fading.[21] The reasons for this situation are several. In a letter to Ellen White, Isaac Van Horn placed some of the blame on Joseph H. Waggoner of California. Van Horn claimed that Waggoner's "public censure" of him at the 1881 camp meeting had "brought gloom and discouragement on the meeting."[22]

Another reason may have been due to William Leavitt, the treasurer who stole a third of the conference's funds during 1880.[23] Though this problem and others had caused the North Pacific Conference to struggle financially, Van Horn claimed in his final report from the Northwest in 1881, that the situation was improving. He wrote: "Financially the conference is recovering from the heavy discouragement it has been wading through the past two years, and the outlook for the future is cheering."[24]

After the 1882 camp meeting, Boyd organized a church of 20 members in East Portland. The previous year, the Burden family had moved from the East to Portland and had started a small Sabbath school for the few scattered believers of the city.[25] The next year, Boyd decided to build up this small church by conducting evangelistic meetings with the new conferences 43- x 60-foot tent at the corner of G Street and 7th Avenue.[26] He also helped the members erect a Tract and Missionary depository building with a reading room for the public near the corner of L Street and Fifth Avenue.[27]

The Portland members leased a lot on G Street between Tenth and Eleventh Avenues in 1883 and erected a church building. Boyd urged them to take a ten-year lease on the lot instead of buying it because Jesus was "coming soon." Ten years later the owners of the lot refused to renew the lease, and the Adventists lost their church building. Though disappointed, the Portland members rallied to erect another structure at N.E. 11th Avenue and Everett Street. This became the Portland Central Church.[28]

In a report to the *Review and Herald* in January 1884, Boyd described the progress in Portland.

Since the tent came here last summer, nine members have been added to the church. . . . A reading room has been built and furnished with reading matter. . . . A church has also been built in a pleasant part of town, and will be open for meetings next Sabbath. . . . We are seeking, by divine grace, to make this [Portland] a central missionary station for this rich and remote corner of God's moral vineyard.[29]

After organizing a church in East Portland in 1882, Boyd held tent meetings in Stayton and then in Scio where ten accepted Adventism.[30] He was assisted by E. W. Barnes.

In 1882, two ministers, Barnes and A. Snashall, from other denominations joined with the Adventist church in the Willamette Valley. Describing Snashall in a report to the *Review and Herald*, R. D. Benham wrote:

Elder A. Snashall, of Portland, Oregon, . . . but lately embraced the third angel's message, by reading of papers and tracts sent him by our Tract and Missionary workers. . . . He has emerged from the ranks of the first-day Adventists . . . He is an earnest and able speaker . . . He and his wife have fully identified themselves with the body, and joined the Beaverton church.[31]

Both men were issued ministerial credentials and rushed into the Adventist ministry within several months. This proved to be a terrible mistake.[32] Within a year, both men began pulling the sympathies of the church members away from Charles Boyd and to themselves. They also turned William Raymond, who was already unstable, against Boyd and the denominational leaders. At some point, Barnes also made contact with the Iowa dissident group, the Marion party, and began promoting their ideas.[33]

Boyd worked hard during his first year in the Northwest, conducting meetings at several locations in the Puget Sound of western Washington Territory as well as in the Willamette Valley.[34] By the 1883 camp meeting, the North Pacific Conference had grown to two churches in the Puget Sound area, Lynden and Renton, and six in western Oregon, Beaverton, Coquille, Damascus, East Portland, Eugene City, and Salem.[35]

After the camp meeting in Beaverton, Boyd's problems with his three assistants and their sympathetic church members increased. Some denominational leaders apparently felt that Van Horn was partially responsible for the problems. To vindicate himself, Van Horn wrote Ellen White.

> Since I left [Oregon] I have kept up a correspondence with Brother Raymond, [Thomas] Starbuck, and [R. D.] Benham. They have all spoken at times decidedly against Elder Boyd's course. In my letters to them I have always expressed sorrow that they could not work in union with Elder Boyd. I have not to my knowledge, sympathized with them against Elder Boyd. I have exhorted them to work in harmony with his plans. I know, my much respected Sister White, that I have said to you and to both Elders Butler and Haskell, that Elder Boyd's work in Oregon was not accepted by leading brethren in the Conference. But was it said in such a way that I gave the idea that I exulted over the state of things and would like to see Elder Boyd make an utter failure? No, I think not. It was simply to inform you of the state of things there which I thought you did not know. No, I do pity Elder Boyd.[36]

During the next season, Boyd continued to hold tent meetings and work with the churches, but the problems only grew worse. In the Spring of 1884, the leaders in California sent John O. Corliss to the Northwest to work with the two discouraged presidents. He, too, was met with decided resistance.[37] By the summer of 1884, the problems in the Northwestern conferences had reached a critical state. Both presidents were being ignored and, at times, ridiculed by church members. False teachings were being spread, a negative attitude towards the General Conference was growing, and Boyd was having to work with three unsupportive assistants. In early 1884, the leaders of the California Conference, realizing the seriousness of the situation, made plans to visit the Northwest and help deal with these problems.[38]

9
The Crisis of 1884

When all the facts already noted are considered, one must admit that some of the problems faced by Northwestern Adventism in the 1880s can be traced to Isaac Van Horn. When he first arrived in the Northwest, he met with unusual success. In three years he raised up five churches with 200 members, but then the situation changed. Confronted by strong-willed church members, an uncooperative brother-in-law for an assistant, and a sick wife, Van Horn relaxed his efforts, and the newly established churches began to flounder and problems soon developed.

Unfortunately, the leaders who followed Van Horn were not strong enough to correct the situation; other problems arose and things continued to deteriorate. Finally, by the summer of 1884, Ellen White and six ministers traveled from California to the Northwest to meet the crisis.[1] First, they attended the Upper Columbia camp meeting in Walla Walla where Colcord was the president. Waggoner wrote his report to the *Signs of the Times*:

> The condition of the people at the commencement was not the most fortunate for a profitable time. Points of doctrine subversive of the message had been introduced and to some extent received. . . . Reports had also been circulated against most of those who are bearing responsibilities in the work . . . [and] by these means a spirit of complaining had been fostered.[2]

Ellen White spelled out one problem in more detail in a letter to Uriah and Harriet Smith:

> Brother Raymond has never been in harmony with his brethren. He has been independent, self-conceited, but carries an appearance of humility. . . . He was talking against the General Conference . . . he

had some new light on Revelation. . . . How we dread to touch this case.

Soon after the California delegation arrived, the men from the Milton church approached them with instructions on what they should preach. Ellen White's letter to the Smiths added:

We heard them respectfully and preached the word of the Lord without any reference to their suggestions. . . . Just as soon as we preached the plain principles of truth there was a buzzing in the camp like a swarm of bees. They said Elder Waggoner and I were clubbing them. . . . I can tell you there was great astonishment and marveling that I dared to speak to them thus.

Sabbath afternoon, William Raymond began to leave the grounds because he felt the delegation from California was "clubbing him." Ellen wrote:

I sent for him. I read to him. I talked with him. I told him that when my brethren, as did Brother Owen, come up with new light he almost made me have an ague chill, for I knew it was a device of Satan. . . . Well, this talk helped the man. . . . The snare was broken. Brother Raymond was balanced in the right direction once more where he could be helped. It will take time to work him out all clear.[3]

The testimony that Ellen White wrote to William Raymond (Brother D) can be found in *Testimonies for the Church*, vol. 5, pp. 289-297. Many other testimonies which pertain to the Northwest can be found in pp. 249-302.

Later the delegation from California listened to Raymond's views on Revelation and gave their reply. He agreed to abide by their decision.[4] In her testimony to Raymond, Ellen wrote:

There are a thousand temptations in disguise prepared for those who have the light of truth; and the only safety for any of us is in receiving no new doctrine, no new interpretation of the Scriptures, without first submitting it to the brethren of experience. Lay it before them in a humble, teachable spirit, with earnest prayer; and if they see no light in it, yield to their judgment; for "in the multitude of counselors there is safety."[5]

Many of the leading members in the small Upper Columbia Conference, especially those from the Milton church, had become critical and unsupportive. Ellen White explained how they dealt with this problem in her letter to the Smiths.

One part of the morning we would declare the true condition of these leading men; then we would change the exercises and have a meeting calling the wrong forward, laboring for them, praying for them. . . . We would have a most remarkable meeting. The Spirit of the Lord was manifested. Then these men would half confess and bear good testimonies, but the grumbling and criticism were in them and they would not keep it from breaking out.[6]

By the end of the Upper Columbia camp meeting, Ellen White was able to write a more positive letter to Uriah Smith.

The meeting closed up well in Walla Walla. It was a success, and a great change has taken place in the feelings of the Upper Columbia Conference.[7]

Next the California delegation traveled to Portland for the North Pacific camp meeting where Charles Boyd was the president. On the way, the train made a 20-minute stop at Multnomah Falls along the Columbia River. Ellen White and the California delegation hiked up to the base of the upper falls. She wrote:

The water pours from the top of a mountain about 900 feet high, and as the water descends, it breaks upon jutting rocks, scattering off in a beautiful spray. Here was the most beautiful sight to look upon. I would have enjoyed it could I have spent an entire day viewing this scene.

In Portland, Ellen found some of the same problems that she had encountered in Walla Walla. The leading men in the conference had "no respect for the General Conference. . . no respect for ministers or president." They were especially harsh with Charles Boyd, the president of their own conference. Ellen described the unfortunate situation to Uriah Smith.

> Brother Boyd was despised by them. Elder Van Horn was a pleasing speaker, and they despised the man [Boyd] because he could not speak as fluently as Elder Van Horn. They contrasted the gifts to his face in the assembly. Brother Boyd has felt [hurt] to the very depths of his soul.

Ellen blamed some of this problem on Van Horn. She wrote: "The mold that Elder Van Horn left upon these two conferences was of that character to make it exceedingly hard for any minister who should follow after him."

Ellen tried to convey in her letter to Smith the intense problems they faced.

> The work in this conference was of the same character as the work above [Upper Columbia], only more so. We had one of the hardest battles we ever had to engage in. . . . The people had no respect for ministers or president. . . . The only thing they did not dare to reject was the testimonies. To these they did bow after long delay.

The stress of the Upper Columbia camp meeting had taken its toll on Ellen. By the time the California delegation had arrived in Portland, she took to her bed with "a burning fever." For the next four days Ellen was unable to leave her tent. On Sabbath, she mustered enough strength to speak for 30 minutes. As the week progressed, the California delegation tried to help the critical members. Then early on Friday morning, Ellen made a prolonged appeal. Concerning this meeting, she wrote:

> I rose and talked a short time telling them we had waited for these leading men to take a position which God could approve and let His Spirit into the meeting. We had no more appeals to make to them. . . . They had stood directly in the way of our work from the first. . . . I had two front seats cleared and asked those who were backslidden from God and those who had never started to serve the Lord, to come forward. They began to come.

What happened next was a miracle. Describing the event, Ellen wrote:

Then the Spirit of God like a tidal wave swept over the congregation. Such solemnity, deep, earnest, heartfelt confessions, were made. These men who had stood like icebergs melted under the beams of the Son of righteousness. . . . Confessions were made with weeping and deep feeling. . . . It seemed like the movement of 1844. I have not been in a meeting of this kind for many years. After the hard fought battle the victory was most precious. We all wept like children.[8]

Nine years later, John Loughborough mentioned that Ellen had a vision at this camp meeting. He wrote:

I have seen Sister White in vision about fifty times. The first time was about forty years ago. . . . Her last open vision was in 1884, on the camp ground at Portland, Oregon. She has visions at the present time, but they are not open visions in a public assembly.[9]

At the North Pacific Conference session, Snashall and Barnes were disfellowshipped. Describing their situation, Waggoner wrote:

The partial acceptance of truth by Elders Snashall and Barnes proved to be a detriment to the work in Oregon. It is always a detriment to the cause in any conference to have ministers in the field who are not thoroughly converted to, and sound in, the faith. . . .

We know of no field which has suffered so deeply because of perverted sympathy [towards Barnes and Snashall and against denominational leaders] as Oregon. But we trust the spell is fully and completely broken.[10]

When the California delegation returned home, only two conference presidents out of the Northwest's six ministers remained. Barnes and Snashall had been disfellowshipped, Alonzo T. Jones had been transferred to the California Conference, and William Raymond had been sent to Healdsburg College in California. Even Colcord, Upper Columbia Conference president, turned over the presidency to Loughborough. The stress of working under such criticism had destroyed his health.[11]

After the East Portland camp meeting, Waggoner wrote a positive report in the *Signs of the Times*:

> It cheers us much to know that a new era has dawned upon the work in the North Pacific Conference. Had a faithful and judicious course been pursued in the past, churches might now dot the Willamette Valley, and the cause be strong in that field. We hope that all may now strive to 'redeem the time' by diligence in every good word and work.[12]

In the five years following the 1884 crisis, the two conferences in the Northwest put into practice this advice. The membership of the North Pacific Conference skyrocketed from 237 to 627; and the membership of the Upper Columbia Conference jumped from 180 to 438. It is true that much of this increase came from Adventists moving into the Northwest to obtain inexpensive land, but a good share of it can also be attributed to the fact that both the membership and leadership of the Northwest turned from their past problems to the task of spreading the message of Adventism.[13]

10
The West Side

The states of Oregon and Washington are divided by the Cascade Mountain Range into two vastly different geographical regions. The eastern portion of both states is lightly populated with small towns separated from one another by semi-arid farmlands, grasslands, and mountain ranges. The western portion, with its wetter climate and dense forests, is more heavily populated. For residents of these states, the western region is often referred to as the West Side.

Adventists in Oregon and Washington Territory decided in 1880 to use these natural geographical regions as the basis of conference territories instead of state and territorial boundaries.

Following the 1884 camp meeting, Charles Boyd and John Loughborough visited the members of the Salem and Scio churches. When they were disfellowshipped, Snashall and Barnes claimed they would "take many of the church" with them. Their boast proved false in Salem but somewhat true in Scio where "some persons were letting go of the Sabbath."[1]

One of the evangelistic methods used by Adventists was the literature rack. These racks were placed in 19 "leading hotels" in Portland and on all of the region's steamboats. After attending the Walla Walla and Portland camp meetings in 1884, William Ings spent several months in the Northwest giving leadership to this work. He reported that Northwestern Adventists were distributing "650 *Signs* per week" as well as selling tracts and pamphlets.[2]

After working with the churches in Salem and Scio, Boyd, along with John Burden his new assistant, took the conference tent to Ashland in the southwestern portion of the state. Though opposition to Boyd's meetings was strong, several families accepted the Sabbath and began holding weekly services.[3]

Concerning the conference, Boyd wrote in 1885, "A degree of union and harmony prevails, which shows plainly that the Spirit of God is working in our midst."[4] In East Portland, Boyd found that the members had started a German-speaking Sabbath school and were having to enlarge their new church building which was "already too small." In two and a half years, the church had grown to nearly 60 members.[5]

When Loughborough visited the West Side in early 1885, he, too, noted the dramatic change in the members' attitude. He stated: "It [spirit of unity and harmony] is in such marked contrast with the state of things that existed one year ago that we can only say, 'What hath God wrought!'"[6] During the spring of 1884, Boyd had conducted evangelistic meetings in West Chehalem Valley, Oregon, and Carrolton, Washington Territory, near present-day Longview. He organized churches in both of these regions as well as in Corvallis, Oregon, the next year.[7]

In 1882, Healdsburg College in California started to serve the Adventists west of the Rocky Mountains. At the North Pacific Conference session three years later, the delegates voted: "The Testimonies by the Spirit of God state in the most emphatic manner that it is displeasing to God to have bungling work done by ministers . . . [it was] therefore resolved . . . to encourage and urge those who expect to labor in the cause to avail themselves of the advantages of the next fall and winter terms at Healdsburg College." They also voted that H. W. Reed and W. C. Ward should attend the college at the end of the summer.[8]

For a few years, several men attended Healdsburg College and began assisting Boyd in his ministerial work. These included R. D. Benham, John Burden, John M. Cole, G. W. Davis, John E. Fulton, H. W. Reed, and W. C. Ward.[9]

In the summer of 1885, the General Conference moved F. D. Starr to the North Pacific Conference, but several months later transferred him to Illinois. While he was in the Northwest, he held tent meetings with assistance from Ward and Cole in Vancouver of Washington Territory and organized a church of 27 members.[10]

That same summer, John Fulton of Minnesota transferred to the

North Pacific Conference where he hoped to regain his health. He continued to struggle with health problems the first year he was in the Northwest. Whenever his condition allowed, he assisted Boyd with meetings and worked with the churches.[11] (John Fulton is not to be confused with his brother's son, John E. Fulton, who later became a prominent missionary and administrator. The Fulton family members frequently were engaged in denominational work, as we shall see later.) John E. Fulton was raised near Salem, Oregon, and attended Healdsburg College in the 1880s. Following graduation, he returned to the Northwest and served as a minister in the North Pacific Conference for several years.[12]

The condition of the North Pacific Conference had improved significantly by the summer of 1886. Tithe and membership had increased, and several ministerial workers had been recruited.[13] Two churches—Eola and Eugene City—had been disbanded, but 13 congregations were still in operation.[14] After the 1886 camp meeting, Charles Boyd spent the rest of the summer season in Seattle and the Puget Sound.

The 1886 tent season found William Potter, who had been transferred from Michigan in 1885, and H. W. Reed conducting tent meetings in Albany, Oregon, where they organized a small church. W. C. Ward and J. M. Cole worked in Gravel Ford, 7 miles from Myrtle Point, Oregon.[15] A number of members from the Coquille church had moved to Gravel Ford and asked for some ministerial help. After five weeks of tent meetings, Ward and Cole were able to organize a church of 12 members.[16] During the winter, H. W. Reed also held a successful series of meetings and organized a church in Harrisburg, Oregon.[17]

In March 1887, the General Conference asked the Boyds and Dores A. Robinsons to start a mission in South Africa. They became the denomination's first missionaries to this continent.

Four years later, Charles experienced health problems which forced the Boyds to return to the United States. He served as president of the Tennessee River Conference for five years. He died in 1898. After his death, Maud Boyd served as a missionary in Australia, and as a Bible instructor in southern California.[18]

In an 1887 camp meeting report, E. W. Farnsworth stated:

The North Pacific Conference shows marks of prosperity and growth. About 150 have embraced the truth the past year. They have had their years of discouragement and trial in the past, and we think it safe to say that many of them have learned valuable lessons which will not soon be forgotten. . . . The brethren expressed many sincere regrets at being deprived of the labors of Brother and Sister Boyd, whose presence, with the blessing of God, has done so much to bring about this state of prosperity.[19]

At the conference session, the delegates asked John Fulton to take the position of president. Being the only minister in the conference with years of experience, he was the natural choice.[20] However, due to health problems, Fulton soon had to relinquish the position and move to the St. Helena Sanitarium in California.[21]

He was replaced by Samuel Fulton, one of his brothers, who was serving as the president of the Tennessee Conference.[22] He, too, struggled with poor health. By the 1889 camp meeting, his condition was such that he, too, resigned and moved to the St. Helena Sanitarium. Unlike his brother, he was unable to regain his health and died one year later.[23]

After Samuel left the area, the General Conference asked Roscoe C. Porter of Iowa to take the presidency, but they soon decided to send him to Minnesota to be the president of the conference there. John Fulton, who had returned to the Northwest after some time at the sanitarium, was asked to resume the position of president. Unfortunately, his health still was not up to the job, and a year later he again resigned for health reasons.[24]

Even though the North Pacific Conference struggled with leadership after the departure of the Boyds, the membership and tithe base continued to grow, mainly due to the large number of young ministerial workers in the conference. There were six ordained ministers at the time in the conference—Samuel Fulton, G. W. Davis, Isaac Morrison, William Potter, H. W. Reed and W. C. Ward. In addition, there were eight licensed ministers.[25]

It may be worthwhile to note the work done by the young workers who carried on despite the poor health and frequent changes in the leadership. In 1887, W. C. Ward, assisted by J. M. Cole and R. D. Benham, conducted tent meetings in Woodburn. They organized a church of 19 members. These Woodburn members immediately erected a church building that was dedicated in December.[26] Several other ministers held meetings and organized a church in St. Johns that same summer.[27]

During the summer of 1888, tent meetings in western Oregon—Roseburg and McMinnville—proved unsuccessful,[28] but later in the season, H. W. Reed was able to raise up a congregation of 14 members in Ilwaco, Washington Territory.[29] Frederick Jorg, just transferred from Nebraska to work with the German-speaking people, organized a German church of 11 members in West Union.[30]

From 1885 to 1889, the North Pacific Conference made strong gains. The membership increased from 237 to 627 and the number of churches from 12 to 26.[31] The conference tithe went from $1,555 in 1885 to $7,205 by 1889. In 1890, it increased to $11,718 which enabled the conference to send $2,500 to the General Conference "to be used in extending the work in any part of the great harvest-field where most needed."[32]

During the summer of 1889, Isaac Morrison, who had been transferred from California in 1887, and William Potter conducted tent meetings in the southern portion of the conference and organized churches in both Grants Pass and Medford; Frederick Jorg raised up a church in Albina.[33]

In 1893 and 1894, Ward and Stover worked in southern Oregon. In a report to the *Review and Herald*, Ward wrote:

In September [1893] we came to Grants Pass and succeeded in erecting a house of worship which this church has so long needed. After our work here we again returned to Ashland and built a meeting-house there. The brethren at both these places are poor, but have worked faithfully to build a house of worship.[34]

In 1890, the delegates to the conference session selected John E. Graham, a layman, to replace the failing John Fulton as the president of the conference. Since the early 1880s, Graham had been operating a fishing business in Ilwaco, Washington. He continued to serve as president until 1894, when he agreed to be the captain of the missionary ship *Pitcairn* which made trips among the South Seas Islands.[35]

Almost every year from 1883 until 1894, Graham served the North Pacific Conference as the president, secretary, or as a member of the Executive Committee.[36] When he returned from his missionary service in 1897, he worked two years more as the business manager and chaplain of the Portland Sanitarium. After 1900, he returned to private business but continued to serve on various conference committees.[37]

W. W. Sharp transferred to the North Pacific Conference in 1890 from Wisconsin and held tent meetings in Eugene. By winter, he was able to organize a church of 18 members. Other churches organized during the 1890 tent season included: Newberg, Vancouver (B.C.), Willamina, and Marquam.[38]

By the 1890s, the Adventist Church in western Oregon was advancing at a respectable rate with steady growth in membership, tithe, and number of churches. All indicators pointed to the fact that a solid foundation had been laid in this region. A foundation that would eventually support one of the strongest conferences in North America.

11
Puget Sound

The vast majority of pioneers who traveled the rugged Oregon Trail during its first 30 years settled in the Willamette Valley, leaving most of the heavily forested regions of western Washington Territory unentered. In the early 1870s this northern area, known as the Puget Sound, continued to be an isolated frontier. Only Seattle and Olympia in the region had more than 1,000 inhabitants. Then, in 1873, the Northern Pacific Railroad made an announcement that promised to change this situation forever. The good news was that it would connect the Northwest with the rest of the United States by building a transcontinental railroad with its western terminus in the Puget Sound.

As soon as the news became public knowledge, the people each of the little frontier towns of the Puget Sound hoped that it would be selected as the railroad's western terminus. They thought Seattle, the largest town and the county seat, probably would be chosen. What they did not know was that the railroad officials wanted to establish a company-owned and controlled town as its West Coast destination.

After visiting the Puget Sound, the railroad officials realized they could never control Seattle, so they chose the small village of Tacoma. It had a good harbor, inexpensive waterfront property, and its small size was ideal to be the railroad's western terminus. This decision struck Seattle a heavy blow. Immediately, residents and businesses packed up and moved to Tacoma. Seattle's population dropped from 1,500 to 500; Tacoma's population soared from 100 to almost 1,500. But, planning a transcontinental railroad is far different from completing it. It took ten years for the railroad to lay the tracks to the Northwest. All during that time Seattle continued to grow and prosper as the area's trade center while Tacoma stagnated. The railroad officials tried to kill Seattle as the Puget Sound's leading city and to replace it with Tacoma, but with the transcontinental railroad still unfinished, they were unable to succeed.

When the Northern Pacific tracks finally arrived in 1883, Tacoma grew tremendously. Within seven years, its population skyrocketed from 1,200 to 36,000. Though Tacoma gave Seattle some stiff competition during this period, it was not able to unseat it as trade center for the Puget Sound. In the 1890s, Seattle became the western terminus for the Great Northern Railroad and the primary outfitting center for the Alaskan gold rush. This provided Seattle with the momentum to surge ahead of Tacoma and become firmly established as the Puget Sound's largest city.[1]

The first attempt by Adventists to evangelize the Puget Sound region occurred in 1880. A. W. Benson, an Adventist book salesman, made a trip to the White River Valley to visit several Adventist families. While in Talbot, a mining town near Seattle, he held some meetings and several people joined with the existing Adventist families to form a small company.[2]

In 1882, Charles Boyd, president of the 123-member North Pacific Conference, and his assistant, William Raymond, spent several months in the Puget Sound. Boyd and Raymond visited the scattered believers in King County and organized Benson's small group as the Renton church. Next, they traveled up north to Lynden where they started a small Sabbath school for the few Adventists in Whatcom County.[3] Describing evangelistic work in western Oregon and Washington Territory, Boyd wrote:

> When I came to this coast, I was told by those who should know that there was but little chance to labor in this Conference during the winter months, on account of mud and rain. I felt much discouraged at such a prospect; but on approaching, I found "the lion chained". . . . There are many more openings than I can meet, notwithstanding the mud and rain.[4]

During the early 1880s, the problems of the North Pacific Conference consumed so much of Boyd's time he was unable to return to the Puget Sound for several years. Finally, in the summer of 1886, he and William Potter returned to the region's trade center, Seattle. During the years Boyd was occupied, this city of 10,000 inhabitants had more than doubled. Four years later, Seattle boasted a population of 42,800.[5]

Boyd and Potter held tent meetings at the corner of Third Avenue and University Street in 1886. The first night, a huge crowd turned out to hear Boyd speak on Daniel 2. The local newspaper, *Seattle Post Intelligencer*, reported that "many stood on the outside."[6]

When Boyd reported to the denominational magazines, he mentioned that Seattle's leading newspapers were reporting on his meetings. During the months of June and July, the *Seattle Post Intelligencer* published 25 favorable articles. In most of these articles, the reporter summarized Boyd's sermon and listed a few texts.

Boyd and Potter moved their tent in August to a different location in Seattle and started another series of meetings. They also organized a Sabbath school of 30 members. In September, Boyd and his assistants conducted a mini-camp meeting for the 54 scattered Adventists of the Puget Sound region. The camp consisted of one large tent and 12 family tents and was located several blocks from Elliott Bay. Two highlights of the gathering were the organization of the Seattle church and a baptism in Lake Union.[7]

During the winter, William Potter and "Brother Anthony" continued to work in Seattle; A. W. Benson conducted Bible studies in Spring Brook (Kent); and Isaac Morrison held meetings in Whatcom County. By summer, their efforts had increased the membership of the Seattle church from 12 to 26. They also established Sabbath schools in Artondale in Whatcom County and at Spring Brook.[8]

While Boyd and Potter worked in Seattle, others were evangelizing elsewhere. The small North Pacific Conference of 301 members sent H. W. Reed and J. A. Burden to the railroad city of Tacoma with its 10,000 inhabitants in the summer of 1877. After several months of tent meetings, the two ministers succeeded in organizing a small church of 13 members. In the fall, conference leaders tried to give this struggling church a boost by holding another mini-camp meeting in Tacoma.[9]

In 1886, the North Pacific Conference assumed the territory of British Columbia. That summer Charles Boyd visited the few Adventists living in the region and organized a Tract and Missionary Society in the provincial capital of Victoria. Three years later, H. W. Reed conducted tent meetings in Victoria and organized a church.[10] The following summer, V. H. Lucas, recently transferred from Ohio, and Isaac Morrison held tent meetings and organized a church in Vancouver, British Columbia—not to be confused with Vancouver in Washington Territory.[11]

At the 1893 General Conference session, Dan T. Jones, district superintendent, urged the delegates to create a separate mission for British Columbia. He suggested that Victoria, where the church members had erected a building, would be a good location for a mission headquarters, but his recommendation was not accepted. The General Conference finally got around to creating a mission for this vast region in 1902.[12]

Isaac Morrison held meetings in the Ridgeway schoolhouse in Skagit County in 1888, and organized a Sabbath school. The next summer, Ward and Cole conducted tent meetings in Aberdeen, and organized a Sabbath school of 15 members.[13]

By the end of the 1880s, a good foundation had been laid in the northwestern corner of the United States. The Puget Sound Adventists had established seven churches and four Sabbath schools and also had erected church buildings in Seattle, Tacoma, and Lynden.[14]

Unfortunately, the momentum of the 1880s did not last. The leadership of the North Pacific Conference based in Portland neglected the Puget Sound region for the next decade. Daniel T. Fero, leader in the "Puget Sound country" during most of the 1890s, hinted at this neglect in an 1896 *Review and Herald* article:

> Seattle is the largest city in the state, having about sixty thousand population. The general work in the field has taken my attention so much that comparatively little has been done in the city. . . . There has been but few laborers in the field [Puget Sound], and yet there is a steady growth. . . . I have been called to Oregon to labor each summer [tent evangelism season], so my time here has been limited.[15]

Perhaps the Puget Sound region was neglected during the 1890s, but note the number of churches established—Wilkeson (1889), Mt.

Vernon (1892), Bellingham (1894), Centralia (1895) Everett (1895), Aberdeen (1896), Elma (1896), Montesano (1896), and Oakville (1897).[16]

An article in an 1894 *Review and Herald* offers a glimpse into the life of one western Washington church located in the mining town of Wilkeson at the base of Mt. Rainier.

> Our church is crowded every Sabbath, and also on Sunday night. We meet Sabbath mornings at six o'clock for prayer meeting, and have such good seasons with the Lord. Then at ten o'clock we have our Sabbath school, followed by a preaching service. At three o'clock a public Bible reading is given. . . . Also all of our company are working from house to house with the tracts, and report good success. We are as busy as bees. We visit evenings after we leave the mines, and I tell you, my brother, we have no time for faultfinding in our church now, because we are so busy working with Jesus.[17]

One of the young ministers of the North Pacific Conference during the 1890s was John E. Fulton. George Fulton, his father, had moved his family in 1875 from Nova Scotia to Oakland, California. Here, George's sister who was a Seventh-day Adventist invited him and his wife to attend evangelistic meetings. George refused, but his wife attended and joined the church. George then moved his family to Oregon to get away from Adventist influences. They settled in a remote region several miles from Salem. Because there were only a few Seventh-day Adventists in western Oregon, George was confident they had escaped from Adventism.

About a year later, George learned that a family was moving onto the property next to theirs. He was glad to get a neighbor, but he wondered what they would be like. Then he heard the shocking news: they were Seventh-day Adventists! Even worse, his new neighbor invited Alonzo T. Jones, a ministerial assistant, to hold evangelistic meetings in town near his homestead. When Jones, the ex-soldier-turned-minister, visited the Fultons, George took a liking to him. As a result, he attended Jones' meetings and later joined the Adventist Church.

It was in this environment that young John E. Fulton, George's son, grew up. In 1886, at the age of 17, John E. traveled to California to enroll in the ministerial course at Healdsburg College.[18] After graduation, John and his new wife, Susie, started working for the North Pacific Conference.[19]

In the summer of 1892, Fulton, along with two young ministers, S. W. Nellis and Joel C. Rogers, traveled to the lumber town of Mount Vernon, Washington. Their goal was to hold tent meetings and raise up an Adventist church. At first the attendance was small, so the ministers held children's meetings in the afternoon with charts and picture rolls. Though attendance at the evening meetings increased somewhat as a result of the children's influence on their parents, it never became large, but Fulton and his assistants still were able to organize a small church in this town of 1,200 inhabitants.

The next year, the Mt. Vernon group erected a modest church building which gave the members a tremendous boost. Then the leaders from the Loud Cry movement (see *Testimonies to Ministers and Gospel Workers*, pp. 15-62) visited Mt. Vernon. They succeeded in convincing several members that all churches, including the Seventh-day Adventist, were Babylon. They even encouraged the members to sell their new building and donate the money to the Loud Cry movement. Fortunately, Mr. Beacraft, who was opposed to this movement, held the deed to the church and refused to sell the building. Had it not been for his courage, the building would have been lost to Adventism. When the conference leaders learned what was going on, they sent John E. Fulton back to Mt. Vernon. He visited the members "day and night" until he was able to restore their confidence in Adventism.[20]

At the turn of the century, Adventist leaders began to realize the need to evangelize more effectively in the Puget Sound region. They saw that the ratio of Adventists to non-Adventists in western Oregon was 1 in 244; in western Washington it was 1 in 395. To correct this situation, they divided the North Pacific Conference into two separate conferences—Western Oregon and Western Washington—with the Columbia River as the dividing line. Under this new organizational arrangement, the new Western Washington Conference more than doubled its membership (975 to 2,374) during the next 13 years.[21]

12
The Inland Empire

The arrival of the railroads in the early 1880s helped the region between the Rocky and Cascade Mountain Ranges to enter a period of rapid settlement. People began referring to the region as the Inland Empire instead of the Upper Country, a title still being used today.[1]

After Adventism's crisis in the Pacific Northwest in 1884, General Conference officials realized they needed a strong leader for the Upper Columbia Conference, someone who could stand up to the independent-minded pioneers on this isolated frontier. In 1885, they asked Henry Decker to move to Walla Walla and serve as the president of this conference with eight scattered churches and 180 members. Since all of the ministers of the Upper Columbia Conference had been transferred after the 1884 crisis, the General Conference sent a new work force into the area to assist Decker—J. Bartlett of Nebraska and J. J. Smith of Wisconsin.[2]

Henry Decker had grown up on the frontier of Wisconsin Territory. He had quickly learned about the hardships and rigors of pioneer life. His father, a circuit-riding Baptist pastor, often was gone ministering to the scattered settlers, so Henry and his brothers and sisters were expected to help their mother maintain the farm.

At the age of 22, Henry attended some Adventist tent meetings in Lodi, Wisconsin. At the end of the series, Isaac Sanborn, the speaker, baptized him. Two years later, he married Nancy Babcock, another Sanborn convert.

At the peak of the Civil War, Decker had entered the Adventist ministry in Wisconsin. That same year, the Adventist leaders selected him as one of the church's representatives to visit Washington, D.C., to seek from government officials a provision for Adventist soldiers to be exempt from bearing arms. Their request was granted.

Decker, son of a preacher and a logical and forceful speaker, proved to be a highly successful minister.[3] At 39, he was elected president of the 1,048-member Wisconsin Conference. At the time, one-tenth of the denomination's members lived in Wisconsin, the second largest conference in Adventism. Under Decker's ten-year leadership, the Wisconsin Conference grew by 50 percent to a membership of 1,525. Only the Michigan and California conferences were larger.[4]

After Decker arrived in the Inland Empire in March 1885, he and John Loughborough, interim president of the Upper Columbia Conference, spent several weeks visiting the churches and the scattered members. Later, he and J. Bartlett traveled to nearby Centerville, Oregon (known today as Athena), and held tent meetings.[5] Because of the problems of the 1884 camp meeting, the General Conference asked E. J. Waggoner to conduct a ten-day Bible institute before the upcoming camp meeting. The gatherings conducted in Milton were marked by a spirit of union and a desire to advance the cause.[6] After the time, the conference was still struggling financially. Progress had been made, but the conference was still in debt.[7]

At the 1885 session, delegates addressed this problem by passing a resolution that "the ministers [should] labor to bring all the churches up to their full duty in the matters of paying tithes." They also voted to "heartily thank" the California Conference for their offer to financially support one minister in the Upper Columbia Conference for an entire year.[8] The next year the tithe increased by 31 percent, thus stabilizing the finances of the conference.[9]

During the summer of 1885, Decker chose William L. Raymond as his tent master. As you may remember Raymond had been one of the key troublemakers in the 1884 crisis. Now he had just returned from a stay at Healdsburg College in California. Decker and Raymond spent the summer months holding tent meetings in Union and Summerville in the Grande Ronde Valley of eastern Oregon.[10]

More help arrived in the person of Daniel T. Fero. Fero had accepted Adventism at the age of 18 about 20 years earlier. Before coming to the Inland Empire, he had served in New York and Pennsylvania, helping to start churches in Pittsburgh and Philadelphia.[11]

Before the completion of the Northern Pacific transcontinental railroad, the eastern portion of Washington Territory was lightly populated. Walla Walla reigned as the hub of the southwestern region, but up north no one village emerged as a center for trade.

Spokane Falls was the oldest town. But in 1880, a group of speculators and railroad men decided to lay out Cheney, a rival village 16 miles to the southwest. The new town soon gained prominence by cornering most of the railroad business and capturing the county seat during a highly disputed election. Then gold was discovered in 1882 along the Coeur d' Alene River in northern Idaho. Spokane Falls, closer to the mines than Cheney, soon became the supply center for the thousands of fortune seekers swarming into the area. This bonanza gave Spokane Falls the momentum it needed to pass Cheney and emerge as the leading town of the region.

The arrival of the Northern Pacific Railroad also encouraged thousands of farmers to travel to the region and settle on the virgin lands in the Palouse Hills. Again Spokane Falls served as the supply center for these farmers as well as the Idaho miners causing it to mushroom during the late 1880s and 1890s.[12]

In the summer of 1886, Henry Decker selected Clarence Ford, recently returned from Healdsburg College, to serve as his tent master. (Clarence Ford had an interesting background that figured in the early days of Walla Walla. We will return to that story in a later chapter.) Decker and Ford held three series of meetings in the Palouse Hills in Washington Territory. One was in Spokane Falls, now a town of 4,000 inhabitants. At the end of the meetings, Decker and Ford established a small company of believers that met in Dr. Harrison's dental office on the corner of Howard Street and Riverside Avenue. The other series of meetings were in Pine City and the railroad town of Cheney; these met with little success.

A church of 17 members was organized in Spokane Falls in 1888. Two years later, the members erected a 30- by 45-foot church building on the corner of Astor Street and Nora Avenue. The Spokane Falls church, later known as the Spokane Central Church, grew rapidly and by 1900 it reached a membership of 140.[13]

In March 1887, the General Conference sent James W. Scoles

from Arkansas to the Upper Columbia Conference to help evangelize the region's rapidly expanding population. After working with the growing Spokane Falls company for several months, Scoles held tent meetings in Moscow in Idaho Territory. He was assisted by Will W. Steward, a young minister who had just returned from study at Healdsburg College. Their successful series led to the organization of a strong church of 23 members in Moscow.

Within a year, this new congregation erected a church building.[14] By the late 1880s, the North Pacific Conference had recruited eight local men for the ministry, while the Upper Columbia Conference had enlisted the services of only four—Clarence L. Ford, Alonzo T. Jones, Will W. Steward, and Edwin L. Stewart. This shortage of ministerial recruits weakened the conference's ability to reach its large territory which embraced roughly one-tenth of the United States' landmass.[15] The Upper Columbia Conference began to have more ministerial prospects when young men began graduating from Milton Academy in 1888."[16]

The site for the 1888 camp meeting for the Upper Columbia Conference was alongside a stream in a cottonwood grove just outside of Dayton. Two large tents and 47 family tents were pitched for the annual event that featured Alonzo T. Jones. In an account of the gathering, E. R. Jones wrote:

> As the themes of righteousness by faith, the love of God, the work wrought in the soul by His power, and the steps necessary to come into union with Christ so that we might by His grace live lives of victory instead of almost constant defeat, were dwelt upon, light came into the minds and gladness into the hearts of all. The feeling of many were expressed by one brother who, after hearing, said he felt like taking a long breath.[17]

Alonzo Jones, co-editor of the *Signs of the Times*, wrote a glowing report of the camp meeting and the progress in the conferences:

> Prosperity has attended the labors put forth in this conference the past year, nearly a hundred additions having been made to the membership. Four new churches were received into the conference.

. . . Three years ago the membership was one hundred and eighty, now it is three hundred and forty-nine. . . . Then the tithes were but $1,400, now they are $3,000.[18]

During the summer of 1888, Henry Decker held two series of meetings and organized a small Sabbath School in the John Day Valley of eastern Oregon. Meanwhile, James W. Scoles conducted two successful series and organized churches in Viola in Idaho Territory and Garfield in Washington Territory.[19] The next year the General Conference transferred Scoles to the Pacific Press and moved Samuel H. Kime of North Carolina and J. O. Beard of Iowa to the Upper Columbia Conference. Kime, a mountain preacher, had been one of the first individuals in North Carolina to join the Seventh-day Adventist Church. He had also erected the denomination's first church building in the South at Banner Elk, North Carolina.[20]

The next the camp meeting for the Upper Columbia Conference was located along the Palouse River near Colfax. Here the Adventists learned that their conference had grown to a membership of 438 in 16 churches.[21]

Adventists in both the Upper Columbia and North Pacific Conferences started academies, in Milton and Portland, in the mid-1880s, and both schools grew rapidly. By 1891, however, the members decided to close these institutions and start a college. The members of the Milton church under the leadership of wealthy and independent-spirited William Nichols pushed for the college to be located in their town. When W. W. Prescott, the education secretary of the General Conference, visited Milton, he felt that another site would be needed for the college. He urged that they follow the successful example of Union College in Nebraska where community landowners had donated acreage, speculating that incoming Adventist families would increase land values. The Milton delegation disagreed with Prescott. They believed that Milton, a temperance town, was the ideal environment for a Christian college.

Henry Decker, the strongest local promoter of the college, agreed with Prescott. He was one of the six members of the locating committee, and he urged the group to locate the college in Walla Walla.

For some time, William Nichols and the influential members of the Milton church resented the fact that they could not manipulate Henry Decker as they had the two previous conference presidents. Incensed that Decker opposed the Milton college site, they became increasingly frustrated and tried to remove him from office.[22] But Decker had been highly successful as president of the conference. Under his seven-year leadership, the number of churches had nearly tripled from 8 to 21 and membership had quadrupled.[23]

When the locating committee finally chose the Blalock farm site near Walla Walla for the college, the Milton faction was furious. To make the locating committee reverse its decision, the Milton group refused to cooperate with the college project and pushed even harder for the resignation of Decker.

Since unity was vital if the risky college project was to succeed, the General Conference asked Henry Decker to resign as conference president. Heeding their counsel, he did so in May 1892. Robert S. Donnell of Missouri was selected to take his place.[24] During the next several years, Decker worked in the Illinois Conference and served as president of the Texas Conference. Five years later, he returned to the Northwest to serve as president of the North Pacific Conference, and held that position until his retirement in 1902. During his presidency, Decker was a strong promoter of the newly established Portland Sanitarium, which grew under his leadership.[25] He also served on the board of Walla Walla College, the institution he worked so hard to launch years earlier. When he retired, Decker returned to College Place and served several terms on the college board. He donated $1,000 in 1908 for a normal school (teacher education) building, and he was often referred to as the "Father of Walla Walla College."[26]

When the Northern Pacific Railroad finished its main line up the Yakima River and over the Cascade Mountains in the mid-1880s, the Yakima Valley settled rapidly. Instead of putting their railroad line through Yakima City, the largest town in the region, railroad officials started the rival town of North Yakima, four miles north. In time, the residents of Yakima City realized they could not compete with a railroad town, so they put their buildings on rollers and moved to North Yakima, which today is known as Yakima.[27]

A series of tent meetings was held in North Yakima in 1894. During the winter, a church was organized and a building partially erected. The next year D. E. Scoles reported in the *Review and Herald*:

> Last June [1895] I located at North Yakima, a city of thirty-five hundred people. . . . It is very windy here, and consequently unsafe to hold tent-meetings, and so the securing of halls is necessary. Two series of meetings have been held in this city since I came here. . . . Our church building is now completed, and we have a Sabbath school of forty-three members.[28]

Hundreds of small towns were started in the Inland Empire by the thousands of incoming settlers in the 1880s and 90s. A few soon developed into large towns and cities, but the vast majority remained small. Hence, most of the churches in the Upper Columbia Conference were small congregations located in rural areas. In fact, of the 12 largest towns and cities in the Upper Columbia Conference today, only five had a Sabbath school or church by the turn of the century.[29]

Today, the Upper Columbia Conference has the highest ratio of Adventists to non-Adventists of any region in the North American Division. One in every 65 individuals in the Inland Empire is a Seventh-day Adventist. The average for the North American Division is one in every 370 individuals. The primary factor for this success is undoubtedly the fact that Adventism entered this region in the frontier period and grew along with it.[30]

13
Father and Son

In the early 1840s, the Pacific Northwest was an untamed wilderness inhabited by a variety of Indian tribes, a few fur trappers, a handful of missionaries, and several hundred American settlers. Maps show the area, claimed by both Britain and the United States, as the Oregon Country.

Dr. Marcus Whitman, a Protestant missionary in the Walla Walla Valley, traveled to the East in 1842. He assured interested Americans that wagons could make the trip to the Northwest even though two other groups had been unable to get any further than Fort Hall near present-day Pocatello, Idaho.

In the spring of 1843, nearly 1,000 Americans in 120 wagons set out for the Oregon Country. After many months of hard work, they finally arrived in the Willamette Valley. The news of their success reached the East, and this inspired others to make the trip. From 1843 until the railroads arrived in the 1880s, large groups of Americans followed the rugged and dangerous Oregon Trail to the Pacific Northwest.[1]

One individual who came with Dr. Whitman in the 1843 wagon train was Ninevah Ford, a young man who had previously moved from his home in North Carolina to the frontier of Missouri in 1840.[2] On the trip to Oregon, Ford's wagon encountered serious trouble at the Snake River crossing. Whitman rushed to his rescue and his timely help kept the wagon from overturning. Later Ford claimed that Whitman had saved his life at the Snake River crossing.[3]

When the emigrants reached the Columbia River, some abandoned their wagons and took small boats or Indian canoes down the river. But Ninevah was determined to get his wagon to the Willamette Valley. With boards from his wagon, he built a raft atop four Indian canoes and placed the shell of his wagon on it. After making a sail from the wagon's cover, he erected a mast in the center of this floating platform. Other emigrants cheered and christened her the "River Queen." Several weeks later, he landed at the small settlement of Oregon City. He was the first person to successfully cross the Oregon Trail in a wagon.[4]

When the Indian wars ended in 1858, the Walla Walla Valley was opened for settlement, and Ninevah Ford moved his family back up the Columbia River to this new frontier.[5] In the 1860s, Ford served three terms as a senator in the state legislature and several terms as a commissioner for the newly established Umatilla County. He allegedly operated the first tannery, shoe shop, and butcher shop in the Northwest and started the first flour mill in the Walla Walla Valley.[6]

Ninevah Ford, resourceful and independent, was a typical pioneer and was noted as a man of strong convictions with little concern for others' opinions. His untrimmed hair and large gray beard gave him a rough appearance, but he was well read and talented in public debate. Ford lived near the main wagon road that crossed the Walla Walla River. When covered wagons stopped for the evening at the crossing, Ford sold them fruit, vegetables, meat, and hay.

Years later the county commissioners decided to have surveyors straighten out the main road between Milton and Walla Walla by moving this wagon road some distance from Ford's house and putting a bridge across the river. Ford fought the decision, but he eventually lost the battle. The night after the new bridge was opened, Ford, several of his family members, and a few of his friends went to work. By using jacks, ropes, chains, rollers, axes, and ten yoke of oxen, they moved the bridge to the river crossing near Ford's house. The next morning the county commissioners were surprised and outraged, but the bridge was never moved back to its original site.[7]

Soon after arriving in the Willamette Valley, Ford and seven other men organized the first Baptist congregation in the Pacific Northwest.[8] Nothing else is known about Ford's early religious life, but in 1874 he attended Isaac Van Horn's tent meetings in Walla Walla and joined the Seventh-day Adventist Church by profession of faith. Eight months later, this independent-minded pioneer became the first Seventh-day

Adventist to be disfellowshipped in the Northwest.[9]

Clarence, one of Ninevah Ford's 11 children, was born in Oregon City two years before his parents moved to the Walla Walla Valley. After attending a frontier public school, he spent several years at Whitman Seminary (now Whitman College). While there, he served as a volunteer with the army in the Nez Perce "uprising."[10]

In 1855, the Nez Perce Indians signed a treaty that gave them a large reservation. When gold was discovered in central Idaho in 1860, the miners and settlers convinced the government to reduce the size of the Nez Perce reservation. The Nez Perce Indians were given a new reservation only one-tenth the size of the original one. Because the new reservation did not include the homeland of some of the bands, they refused to sign the new treaty. In 1877, the government told the non-treaty Nez Perce Indians that they had one month to travel to the new reservation or the U.S. Army would forcibly move them. On their way to this reservation, a group of young warriors killed 18 whites. General Oliver Howard responded by sending Captain David Perry and 103 enlisted men to the Salmon River area where the murders had taken place. At White Bird Canyon, the non-treaty Indians routed the soldiers. Thirty-four soldiers were killed without a single Indian fatality. It was the U. S. Army's second most disastrous defeat by Indians. Only Custer's massive defeat, 225 fatalities, in 1876 at the Little Big Horn River in Montana Territory was worse.

The news struck fear into the hearts of settlers throughout the Northwest. Many wondered if other tribes would join the rebellion. As the settlers became panic-stricken, they rushed to the nearest towns; some frontier communities erected fortresses.

Before conducting a campaign against the insurgent Indians, General Howard brought in troops and volunteers from Walla Walla. Clarence Ford was among these volunteers. Five days later, Howard began pursuing the hostile Indians with a force that eventually grew to over 500. Though Howard was a Civil War hero and the sixth ranking general in the U. S. Army, the Indians led him on a wild goose chase. Once they even circled behind him and cut off his supply lines.

When the Indians headed across the Bitterroot Mountains into Montana Territory to escape to Canada, the volunteers from Walla

Walla were sent home. Three months later a force of 2,000 soldiers finally corralled the renegade Indians only 42 miles from the Canadian border and safety.[11]

The next year Clarence and his older brother settled on adjoining homesteads in the Palouse Hills of eastern Washington Territory. Here they raised horses and mules.[12] Clarence married Minnie Wood, the daughter of James F. and Caroline Wood, in 1881. She had just returned from two years at Battle Creek College. She and her family had been the first Adventists from the Northwest to attend the college.[13]

Even though his parents had joined the Seventh-day Adventist Church in 1874, Clarence had never become a member. Four months after his marriage, he joined the church through baptism at the Upper Columbia Conference camp meeting in Dayton.[14] Soon after, Clarence felt a call to the ministry. The leaders of the 180-member Upper Columbia Conference recognized his talent and issued him a license to preach. That first summer he served as tent master for George Colcord in Goldendale where a small church was started; the next season he helped with meetings in Colfax.

In late 1885, the Clarence Fords with Will W. Steward traveled to Healdsburg College in California to better prepare themselves for the ministry. Seven months later they were called back to Washington Territory to help with camp meetings and evangelism. Ford became tent master for Henry Decker, the new conference president from Wisconsin. During the next tent season they held meetings in Spokane Falls, Cheney, and Pine City. The group they started in Spokane Falls grew into a church of over 100 members within ten years.[15] Then Ford worked at his ranch near Pullman and sold Adventist books for two years. His best success came with *Bible Readings for the Home Circle*.[16]

The Fords served the Upper Columbia Conference in a number of ways. Minnie operated the Tract and Missionary office in College Place from 1892 to 1897; Clarence helped with evangelistic meetings and served as chaplain for the Spokane and, later, for the Walla Walla Helping Hand Missions. During this period, he was ordained to the gospel ministry.[17]

A number of Clarence's brothers and sisters also became Seventh-day Adventists. One of them, C. E. Ford, was a Methodist minister for ten years before he joined the Adventist Church. Then he served as an Adventist minister in the Northwest and California.[18] The Clarence Ford family moved to Newport, Washington, in 1901, where Clarence continued to serve as a minister, helping to establish new congregations in the northeastern portion of Washington and the northern section of Idaho.[19]

Though Ninevah Ford and his son Clarence were different in many ways, they had one thing in common. They were both pioneers. One helped to settle the Wild West; the other introduced its settlers to Jesus Christ.

14

Snake River Adventism

By 1860 most of the Northwest's 64,000 inhabitants resided in the Willamette Valley of western Oregon. Except for small pockets of settlers in the Walla Walla Valley and Puget Sound, the Northwest remained an unsettled wilderness.[1]

That situation changed rapidly in 1860 with the discovery of gold in what is today the state of Idaho. Within three years, nearly 35,000 fortune seekers moved into this unsettled region. One supply center, the newly established town of Idaho City, even boasted a population larger than Portland—the center of trade and transportation in the Northwest.[2]

At first, the miners concentrated their efforts along the Clearwater and Salmon River drainages, but two years later when several prospectors discovered the precious metal in the Boise Basin of southern Idaho, this new region became the focus of the Idaho gold rush.

Fort Boise, a military post, was established in 1863 for this southern mining region. Soon, Boise City sprang up near the fort. Within a year, over 1,500 inhabitants lived in the town which became the capital of the newly established Idaho Territory.

After the gold rush, Boise City became a center of trade, agriculture, and government. In its new role, it grew at a more modest rate, and even as late as 1890, Boise City had only 2,311 inhabitants.[3]

During their first ten years in the Northwest (1874-1883), Adventist ministers directed most of their efforts toward the Walla Walla and Willamette Valleys. Only after the crisis of 1884 did they begin to evangelize southern Idaho Territory, Montana Territory, eastern Oregon, southwestern Oregon, and western Washington Territory. During the nine months between the 1884 camp meeting and the arrival of Henry Decker, new president of the Upper Columbia Conference, John Loughborough served as the interim president of this frontier conference. Late in 1884 he visited a number of the scattered believers in the Washington and Idaho Territories. One of his stops was in Boise City where he stayed with an Adventist physician, Dr. S. Pope, and organized a Sabbath school.[4]

Describing his frustrating trip to Idaho Territory from the eastern portions of Washington Territory, Loughborough wrote:

> Brother W. R. Jones, clerk of the [Farmington] church, came with a team to fetch me to this place [Cheney, Washington Territory], so that I might take the first morning train, and have ample time to perform the trip to Boise City, a place to be reached as yet only by alternate railroading and staging. We traveled most of the night, coming a distance of forty-seven miles, arriving here more than half an hour before the advertised time of the train, but only to learn that this morning the train had received orders to run two hours before its advertised time. So the train, which we had made such an effort to reach, had departed. Here I am in the Northern Pacific Railroad station at Cheney, to wait ten hours for a train. Waiting is one of the tedious parts of railway travel and requires patience. So does it require patience to wait properly for the return of the Lord from Heaven.[5]

A week later, he wrote:

> Including twenty-four hours waiting for trains, I was four and one-half days performing the journey to Boise City, where I arrived on the morning of Sept. 12, having traveled by railroad 400 miles, and by stage 140 miles.[6]

During the 1884 crisis, most of the ministers in the Northwest were disfellowshipped or transferred. So early in 1885, the General Conference sent a new set of workers to the two Northwestern conferences. When the new work force arrived, J. J. Smith was assigned to the unworked region of southern Idaho Territory. Here he more fully organized the Sabbath school in Boise City and raised up a small Sabbath school in High Valley. Then, suddenly, in November 1885, he died of peritonitis at the age of only 42.

Immediately, Daniel T. Fero was sent from Pennsylvania to Boise City to take Smith's place. In early 1886, Fero held meetings and raised up a Sabbath school in Franklin, 20 miles down river from Boise City. The same year he organized the Boise City 22-member and Franklin 17-member groups into two churches. The next year he organized a church for High Valley.[7] In 1891, the members of the Boise City church purchased a house at Thirteenth and State Streets and transformed it into a church. About that time, James and Ellen Casebeer made plans to move from Nevada to Idaho. While still in Nevada, Ellen dreamed she saw a church building, and the Lord said to her: "This is the church that I want you to join." When the Casebeers arrived in Boise City, Ellen saw the Seventh-day Adventist church building and said to her husband: "This is the church the Lord showed me. This is the church we must join."

After studying the Bible with one of the church members, they were baptized. James was well educated and had been a justice of peace in Iowa and a school teacher in Nevada, so his talents were a real blessing to the infant church in Boise City.[8]

Another individual who joined the Adventist Church in the Boise Valley was Mrs. Frank Steunenberg. Her husband served as the governor of Idaho from 1897 to 1901. During his second term, disgruntled miners in northern Idaho hijacked a Northern Pacific train and traveled to the Bunker Hill and Sullivan mines. There they burned and blew up buildings and equipment, with the damage estimated at half a million dollars. Governor Steunenberg sent in federal troops to round up the miners who were placed in a makeshift prison. Because of this action, Steunenberg was hated by the miners' union.

In 1905, a violent miner named Harry Orchard who had strong ties with the leaders of the miners' union attached a bomb to the gate of Steunenberg's home in Caldwell. When the ex-governor arrived home, the bomb exploded and he was killed. The trial that followed drew national attention. Carlos Schwantes, a professor of history at the University of Idaho, suggests that it was "the most sensational trial in Pacific Northwest history."

During the trial, Harry Orchard claimed that he had been hired

f the Western Federation of Miners (miners' union) to
. Eventually, the officials were acquitted, but Orchard
hang. His sentence later was reduced to life in prison.[9]
ın nis autobiography, Orchard related an incident that took place on the
day he was to be hanged. He wrote:

> Julian Steunenberg, son of the former governor whom I had
> murdered, asked Warden Whitney if he might see me a minute. . . .
> The warden came in and told me of the request and also said that
> young Steunenberg had a package in his pocket that looked like a
> gun. He suggested that perhaps I had better not see him. After a
> moment's thought I told the warden that I felt I should see him, and
> that if he wanted to kill me, I guess that, from a human standpoint,
> he had a right to do so.
>
> He came up to me and put out his hand, which I took reluctantly,
> as I felt that I was too much a moral leper to shake hands with him.
> His "gun" proved to be a roll of papers and tracts which he said his
> mother—the wife of the man I had assassinated—had sent to me
> with the request that I read them and turn to God for forgiveness
> and the salvation of my soul.[10]

After this experience, Mrs. Steunenberg began sending letters and
books to Harry Orchard at the penitentiary. In 1909 she requested a
visit. Orchard wrote back and said: "I am so unworthy, and I am
overcome with grief when I think of meeting you face to face."

After seeing her on four occasions by 1913, he wrote:

> I do not feel that awful condemnation that I used to feel in your
> presence. . . . I cannot get over the feeling of sadness and remorse
> when I think of you and your family. While I have not a doubt in the
> world but that you freely forgive me all the sorrow that I caused you,
> I wish I could in some way make it right.

As a result of Mrs. Steunenberg's efforts and those of others, Harry
Orchard became a Seventh-day Adventist Christian.[11]

During the late 1880s and early 90s, Daniel T. Fero, living in the
Walla Walla Valley, supervised the Adventist work in southern Idaho.

In a *Review and Herald* article (1888) he wrote: "I hope the time will soon come when southern Idaho can have continued labor [full-time minister] to develop the work."[12] Fero coordinated small camp meetings for the believers in southern Idaho; one of them in 1887 was held in Franklin, near Caldwell.[13]

Late in 1891 Dan T. Jones, district supervisor for the West Coast region, visited southern Idaho and sent in a report describing the three churches.

During the past summer the company [church] at Boise City has built a very neat and respectable meetinghouse. . . . The unconstrained manners and hospitality characteristic of society on the frontier makes one feel at home on short acquaintance. . . . [Next, we] made a short visit to Highland Valley, a small settlement in a little valley in the mountains, fourteen miles from Boise City. There are but seven families in the valley, five of whom are Sabbath-keepers. . . . [Next] we went to Nampa, and from there five miles into the country to visit the Franklin church. This company has gone through severe trials in the past, but seems, through the help of God, to be coming out of them.[14]

The Adventist Church experienced little growth in the late 1880s and 1890s in the Snake River region. In 1894, Will W. Steward sent a report to the *Review and Herald* that gives us a clue as to why this happened: "In a short time [mid-1880s] we had three organized churches, but false brethren who came in to spy out our liberty which we have in Christ Jesus soon brought in dissension, and as a result the Lord's children became discouraged."[15]

In late 1895, William F. Martin made a similar observation.

The work here has had a great many drawbacks. A spirit of fanaticism had hindered the cause to quite an extent, and things had been allowed to run at loose ends. . . . Reproach has been brought on the cause time and again . . . yet there are several good, staunch souls that hold up the standard of truth.[16]

Another reason for the slow progress in this region was its distance from the conference headquarters in College Place, Washington.

The formation of the Idaho Conference in 1907 caused some financial problems for southern Idaho and eastern Oregon believers, but it solved the distance problem. Actually, this small conference doubled both its membership and the number of churches within the next 20 years.[17]

Even though several series of meetings were held in the Grande Ronde Valley in 1875 by Isaac Van Horn and in other areas through the 1880s, it was not until the 1890s that the Adventist Church was able to establish permanent churches in the portion of eastern Oregon that became part of the Idaho Conference. Except for a short-lived church in Lostine, Wallowa County, the first Seventh-day Adventist church to be established in this region was in 1893 in Union.[18] In a few years, this church had erected a "good church building, facing one of the principal streets . . . a neat structure" that was "lighted by electricity."[19] The Union church continued to be the largest Adventist church in this region until the 1930s. Other early churches in the Idaho Conference portion of eastern Oregon included Long Creek in 1896, Baker City in 1897, and La Grande in 1898.[20]

The Adventist Church in this region faced its greatest challenges in the southwestern and south central portions of Idaho—an area that had been settled by Mormons from Utah. After holding meetings in Idaho Falls in 1898, William F. Martin wrote: "The majority of the people are Mormons, and it seems almost impossible to get them out to meetings."[21] When southern Idaho and eastern Oregon were formed into a conference in 1907, most of the churches were still located in either Oregon or the Boise Valley area.[22] Even today few Adventist churches are located in the southeastern and south central sections of Idaho, where the population is largely made up of Mormons.

More than one hundred years have passed since the arrival of Van Horn in La Grande and J. J. Smith in Boise City. During this time the Seventh-day Adventist Church has grown to over 5,000 members in the Snake River region.[23]

15
Reading, Writing, and Arithmetic

Sabbatarian Adventists in the 1850s and 60s saw little need for their own schools. Because of their belief in the imminent return of Jesus Christ, they felt their limited resources should be invested in warning others. However, as the young denomination rapidly grew, this attitude changed. Leaders saw how church-operated schools could help prepare workers to spread the Advent message.

In January 1872, Ellen White received her first vision concerning education. In her testimony, she called for "a school where those who are just entering the ministry may be taught at least the common branches of education and where they may also learn more perfectly the truths of God's word for this time."[1] Later that year, the General Conference started a small school in Battle Creek, Michigan. With Sidney Brownsberger leading out, the young institution grew rapidly and in just eight years the school had 490 students enrolled.

Ellen White believed the school's primary goal should be to prepare workers for the church. She also urged the teachers to incorporate religious and manual training in their curriculum. The teachers, however, were unfamiliar with vocational and religious education, so they provided the students with a traditional curriculum based on the classics. Therefore, a large number of students who graduated became public school teachers; few chose to work for the church.

When W. W. Prescott took over as president of Battle Creek College in 1885, the institution made slow but steady progress towards implementing Ellen White's reforms.[2]

Battle Creek College was located in the Midwest, so Adventists on both coasts decided in 1882 to start schools of their own. Members in California launched Healdsburg College. There the enrollment rose from 26 to 152 during the first year. In New England, church members established South Lancaster Academy in Massachusetts.[3]

From a financial standpoint, it would seem that the next post-elementary denominational schools should have sprung up in conferences with one to two thousand members—Indiana, Iowa, Kansas, Minnesota, Ohio, and Wisconsin, but this was not the case. In 1886, it was the small conferences of the Northwest, Upper Columbia with 240 members and North Pacific with 301 members, that founded Adventism's fourth and fifth post-elementary schools.[4] Although Healdsburg College had been started to serve the educational needs of the entire West Coast, Northwestern Adventists wanted their younger children to have educational institutions closer to home. The start of academies in the Northwest undoubtedly made the leaders of Healdsburg College nervous. The members of the North Pacific Conference put these leaders at ease at their 1886 session when they made a motion that clearly stated their intent to start an academy in East Portland.

> We indorse the action of the Conference Committee in establishing a school in East Portland . . . the object [of the academy] being not to instruct those who should have the benefits of Healdsburg College, but to prepare persons to receive its instruction, and to rescue our children from the evils of the public schools, and give some help to those not able to attend Healdsburg College.[5]

The first request to start an academy in the Upper Columbia Conference came in 1882 from Alonzo T. Jones and the members of the Farmington church in Washington Territory. Though the delegates at the conference session refused the proposal, they felt that a school should be started in the future.[6]

Two years later, a group of members from the Milton church requested and received permission to open an academy in their area. They invited their former conference president George Colcord to serve as the school's principal and he agreed.[7]

Milton Academy grew rapidly; the school opened with 14 students and had 23 by the end of the first year. The second year the enrollment more than doubled. A three-story dormitory building was erected in 1888 to hold 100 students. At its peak (1890), Milton Academy boasted an enrollment of 150 students.

The academy had three departments of instruction: a six-year elementary course, a four-year academy (high school) course to prepare students for college, and a normal course to train teachers.[8] Students who wanted to receive the teacher's certificate were required to "complete the third year of the academic course, and demonstrate their fitness for teaching, by conducting satisfactorily one class for ten weeks, and answer correctly 80% of all questions asked in the regular examinations on first and second year work."[9]

The members of the Portland church brought Carrie Mills from the East in 1885 to start a school in their church building. Within a year, they hired another teacher, Frank Bunch, to keep pace with the expanding enrollment. The next year the delegates at the North Pacific Conference session voted to turn this East Portland school into an academy. Thomas H. Starbuck, an elder of the Salem church with public- school teaching experience, was asked to direct the project. He sold his farm in early 1887 and solicited funds and erected a two-story school building at NE Nineteenth Avenue and Pacific Street. This 26- by 44-foot structure with a 28- by 18-foot wing cost $2,600.

Sixty-one students attended the first year; the next year 85 attended. Before the academy closed to make way for Walla Walla College, the enrollment reached over 100.[10] The 1889 calendar shows the school year ran from October 21 to April 4. Tuition was $2.00 per month for younger students and $3.00 per month for older students. The board was $2.25 per week.[11] In a *Signs of the Times* report, the philosophy of the school was set forth.

> The intention is to have a school where God will be feared and his word and authority reverenced. It is not intended for the reformation of the wayward, but for the benefit of those who intend to form characters for Heaven. If reformation is needed, it should be well begun at home before entering this school. The common branches, including book-keeping and physiology, will be taught. Instruction in the Bible will also be given. . . . No pains will be spared to make the moral influences of the highest order. . . . Any influences

antagonistic to moral culture and religious training will be strictly prohibited.[12]

The delegates voted at the 1889 North Pacific Conference session to erect a "boarding-house or student home" at their academy or to sell their "present school property on the best terms possible, and obtain a suitable site."[13] By June of the next year, the East Portland school building had been sold and a site had been selected in St. Johns (northwest of Portland) where an $8,000 to $9,000 building was to be erected.[14]

In early 1890, the leaders of the Milton Academy suggested to the General Conference that both academies should be closed and a college started. John E. Graham, president of the North Pacific Conference, opposed the idea. He thought the Upper Columbia Conference, more centrally located to Idaho and Montana than his conference, would undoubtedly be the site for the new college.[15] When Ellen White learned of Graham's opposition, she sent him a letter that changed his thinking.

> I would feel sad indeed to see two schools established, one in Oregon and one in Upper Columbia, it is so contrary to the light which God has been pleased to give me. If you have a school, you want to make it the best that both conferences, with their united means and talents, shall be able to secure. . . . Will you lay aside all selfish interests, and all sectional feelings, and manifest your missionary zeal to work for the best interest of the cause of God? Will you put away all strife in the matter, and show that we are all one in Christ Jesus?[16]

In late 1890 General Conference president, O. A. Olsen, visited the two Northwestern conferences and both groups voted to "unite their school interests."[17]

When the citizens of Milton learned that the Adventists might close their two academies and start a college, they voted to raise funds to purchase another building site for the Adventists in the Milton area. A report of this meeting in the *Milton Eagle* stated:

> A large denominational publishing house will soon follow with many other industries, making Milton another Battle Creek. Prosperity

follows this thrifty and industrious society wherever they cast their lot, and with their permanent establishment in Milton nothing more is needed to assure its rapid growth into the principal city of eastern Oregon.[18]

However, W. W. Prescott, General Conference education superintendent, and the locations committee preferred a 40-acre plot, donated by a non-Adventist physician, west of Walla Walla. As a result, the Milton site was rejected and the new college was located near Walla Walla.[19]

In addition to these schools, the James Bunch family operated a privately owned school in Coquille, Oregon. Later this school became an academy with an enrollment of 140 students. The Bunch children, prepared for the teaching profession at Healdsburg College in the 1880s, taught the courses. The academy closed in 1897 and the buildings were sold to the Methodists. Another Adventist academy, Gravel Ford Academy, was opened in the early 1900s and operated in the area for several years.[20]

The educational system of the Adventist Church consisted of only a few regional institutions during the 1880s and early 90s. The concept of small church-operated schools had not yet taken hold. Only 18 elementary schools were in operation by the denomination in 1895. But in 1897, an education reform movement hit the campus of Battle Creek College. The new president, Edward Sutherland, who had been serving as the first president of the newly established Walla Walla College, led a reform movement urging students to prepare for the teaching profession so that Ellen White's counsel to start small church schools could be implemented. As a result, the denomination had 220 church schools in operation by the turn of the century.[21]

When Ellen White returned from Australia in 1900, she published the sixth volume of the *Testimonies for the Church*. Nearly 100 pages in this volume focused on educational reform. Three years later she also published *Education*. This emphasis, along with the church-school movement, inspired Adventists everywhere to establish elementary and secondary schools. The beginnings of the present Adventist educational system began to emerge.

During the early 1900s, most conferences tried to establish an academy within their own territory. Quite a number of academies were started in the Northwest. Some flourished and developed into institutions that are still operating today; others merged with other institutions or simply faded away.[22] Through the years, many changes have taken place in Adventist education, but one thing remains the same. Adventists in the Pacific Northwest are still committed to providing their children with quality Christian education through a system of church schools, regional academies, and a college.

16
Conard Hall—
The Rest of the Story

For many folks from the Northwest, no place induces more fond memories than Walla Walla College, an institution where they "got educated."

Many alumni pleasantly recall the buildings on campus—Administration Building, Smith Hall, Kretschmar Hall, Village Hall, Sittner Hall, and, of course, Conard Hall, the one building that has produced more memories than all the others. Thousands of couples can recall meeting and saying goodnight on the steps of this building. And how about the fish pond in front of Conard Hall? For many years, Sittnerites (residents of the men's dormitory) would be tossed into the pond when fellow Sittnerites learned that they had become engaged. I will never forget the cold December night when my "friends" threw me into the air and I broke through the ice and splashed into the icy waters of this pond.

Conard Hall, like many of the buildings on campus, was named after an individual who served at the college. In this case, it was Helen Clara Conard, whose story is both amazing and interesting.

In 1852, Helen's father, Alvin Clark, and nine other families started the long journey to the Northwest along the Oregon Trail. Alvin was captain of the wagon train, so his wife Mary had to drive their wagon in addition to watching their eleven-month-old twins—Helen and Clarence. One day, after the group had been traveling for about two months, the children began playing Indians with miniature bows and arrows. They were having a great time when suddenly an arrow hit one of Mary's oxen. Terrified, the animals began running wildly with the wagon bouncing behind them.

Mary realized that the wagon would probably overturn. She gathered her babies in her arms and jumped. At just that moment, a young man from another wagon train rode his horse right beside her wagon. He leaped from his horse the second Mary jumped and caught her midair in his arms. All four of them rolled across the hard ground and through the sagebrush. When the dust lifted, they discovered that no one, not even the babies, was hurt. Mary and Alvin both thanked the young stranger who was on his way to the gold fields of California.[1]

The Clarks initially settled in Oregon, but moved in 1862 to a homestead at Brush Prairie, about ten miles north of Vancouver in Washington Territory. After Helen graduated from the frontier school near her parents' homestead, she attended an academy in Portland and spent a year preparing for the teaching profession. For the next few years, Helen taught rural schools in the area north of Vancouver.[2]

While teaching at the Douthit schoolhouse, Helen began seeing a forty-year-old man named George. One day after school they were chatting while sitting on the steps of the schoolhouse and the subject of horses came up. George told Helen that his favorite horse was a black stallion that he had ridden to California along the Oregon Trail. He began relating to Helen a story about this horse and the trip he had taken in 1852. He told her that one day he saw a wagon from another wagon train rushing wildly across the plain. He spurred his black stallion hoping he could stop the wagon before it overturned. Just as he came alongside, the woman jumped with two babies in her arms. He also leaped from his horse and managed to catch them in midair. At this, Helen could not keep silent. She told George that the woman he had caught was her mother and she was one of the twin babies.

In May of 1876, George Conard and Helen Clark were married. Nine years later they attended evangelistic meetings held by Charles L. Boyd, then president of the North Pacific Conference, and joined the Seventh-day Adventist Church.[3]

They moved to Milton, Oregon, in 1890 so their children could attend Milton Academy. Two years later they relocated to the newly established town of College Place, Washington. The house that George Conard built that year (1892), at the corner of Fourth Street SE and Birch Avenue SE, is one of the oldest buildings in College Place.

Two years later, and at the age of forty-three, Helen enrolled at Walla Walla College. Four years later, in 1898, she and Ada, her oldest daughter, comprised half of the college's third graduating class from Walla Walla College. For the next ten years, Helen served on the staff of the college in many capacities, as preceptress (dean of women), librarian, history and English teacher, and intermediate school teacher.[4]

When Walla Walla College erected a women's dormitory on the east side of College Avenue in 1934, it seemed only natural to name it Conard Hall. Two additions were made to this brick structure in 1954 and 1960 making it one of the largest buildings on campus.[5]

17
Big Sky Country

Gold was the magic word in the Wild West. News of its discovery in a new location could trigger a stampede of miners that almost overnight could transform a remote valley into a boomtown. During the early 1860s, gold rushes along the Clearwater, Salmon, and Boise rivers of Idaho Territory lured thousands of miners into the northern Rockies. In time, these explorers for gold traversed into the mountains of western Montana and discovered more evidence of the precious metal. As word leaked out, thousands of prospectors swarmed to this newly discovered bonanza.[1] Despite this, Montana remained an isolated wilderness for many years. Its semi-arid grasslands and its tribes of hostile Indians made it unattractive to the settlers.

When the Northern Pacific Railroad arrived in Montana in the early 1880s, it began to experience growth. By 1890, its population reached 142,924, but many of these early settlers were ranchers who grazed large herds of cattle on the open range,[2] and, of course, the gold miners.

The General Conference leaders believed that evangelistic work should be started in this rapidly growing region as soon as possible. They assigned Montana Territory in 1886 to the Upper Columbia Conference. With all of Idaho and Montana Territories plus the eastern portions of both Oregon and Washington Territory, this small conference of 240 members and four ministers was overwhelmed. The conference did not possess the resources to evangelize a region of over 325,000 square miles (a region equal to Illinois, Indiana, Iowa, Michigan, Missouri, and Ohio). Consequently, Montana Territory was neglected.[3]

In the summer of 1888, the General Conference sent O. A. Johnson from Nebraska to Montana Territory to conduct tent meetings.

He located in the Livingston area, now near Yellowstone National Park. When he left Montana Territory in November, he reported he had organized one Sabbath school of 20 members in Livingston and another of 15 members "in the country about seven miles from the city."[4]

In an effort to establish an Adventist presence in Montana Territory, the following year the General Conference officials made the region a mission under their direct supervision. They sent Daniel T. Fero of the Upper Columbia Conference to oversee the work. Fero traveled from Walla Walla to Montana during the summer. He held tent meetings in Bozeman, a town of 3,500, but met with minimal success.[5] The next year, J. W. Watt of Missouri was asked to go to Montana. Watt was like Elisha who had been called into the ministry as a young boy while plowing in a field. Watt became the superintendent of the Montana Mission. Also sent was Eugene Williams, an unordained minister from Michigan, to assist Watt in his evangelistic work.

The two ministers started by organizing the Livingston group as a church. Then, as soon as the group finished building its new church, a series of meetings was conducted. More meetings were held at Short Hill (about 18 miles from Livingston), Townsend, and the mining town of Virginia City, where a Sabbath school was "partially" organized.[6] The next summer, the ministers held tent meetings at two locations in Bozeman. Though attendance "was not large at any time," several accepted their message and a church of 12 members was organized.[7]

Watt and Williams made slow but steady progress in the 1890s. Their meetings brought only a few individuals into the church, but the Montana Mission moved forward. Their first camp meeting held in 1892 could boast 125 attendees.[8] Dan T. Jones, district superintendent of the West Coast, and Eugene W. Farnsworth, district superintendent of the upper Midwest, attended the Bozeman camp meeting. Farnsworth wrote to the *Review and Herald*.

It was a small meeting, there being only fifteen small tents and two large ones. About seventy-five of our people were in attendance. This meeting reminded me of many camp meetings attended years ago in Dakota, Nebraska, and other states, when the truth first began its work in those places.[9]

Watt held meetings in Helena, the state capital, the fall of 1892. There he organized a Sabbath school of 20 members. He also organized a church of nine members in Belgrade, a small town near Bozeman.[10] Also, in 1892 the General Conference chose Charles N. Martin, an unordained minister from the Upper Columbia Conference, to join Watt and Williams in Montana. Martin had become an infidel at the age of 14 when he was left alone at his mother's death. A teacher at Milton Academy had introduced him to Adventism. After graduating, he married one of the teachers, Cora Peabody, and entered the ministry.[11]

Several years after losing his six-year-old girl and eleven-month-old boy to scarlet fever, A. W. Stanton, a member of the Livingston church, became one of the five members of the Montana Mission Committee. Stanton decided to sell his ranch and livestock for $40,000 and to donate the money to the denomination. Several unfortunate encounters with church workers, however, made him change his mind. He became increasingly critical toward the church leadership. By 1892, he started to promote some unorthodox views concerning the Seventh-day Adventist Church. Watt and Dan T. Jones tried to reason with him, but Stanton would not listen.[12] He stopped returning his tithes and persuaded a number of others in the small Montana Mission to do the same. He even convinced Williams, Watt's assistant, that his own teachings were of God.[13]

When Ellen White heard about Stanton's views all the way in Australia, she sent him a letter. She wrote:

> My brother, I learn that you are taking the position that the Seventh-day Adventist Church is Babylon, and that all that would be saved must come out of her. You are not the only man the devil has deceived in this matter.
>
> I understand that you are also proclaiming that we should not pay tithe. My brother, take "off thy shoes from off thy feet"; for the place whereon you are standing is holy ground. The Lord has spoken in regard to paying tithes. He has said, "Bring ye all the tithes into the storehouse." . . . God has a church upon the earth who are His chosen people, who keep His commandments. He is leading, not

stray offshoots, not one here and one there, but a people.[14]

This message by White was later published in *Testimonies to Ministers and Gospel Workers*.

In 1893 Stanton published a small pamphlet entitled *The Loud Cry of the Third Angel's Message*. He sent copies to Seventh-day Adventists throughout the United States. In it he concluded that the Seventh-day Adventist Church had become Babylon and that the faithful should separate from the church.

Ellen White responded to Stanton's pamphlet with a series of articles in the *Review and Herald*. These messages were reprinted in *Testimonies to Ministers and Gospel Workers*, pp. 15-62.[15]

> I have been made very sad in reading the pamphlet that has been issued by Brother S. [Stanton] and by those associated with him in the work he has been doing. Without my consent, they have made selections from the Testimonies, and have inserted them in the pamphlet they have published, to make it appear that my writings sustain and approve the positions they advocate.[16]

In another article concerning Stanton, White wrote:

> When men arise, claiming to have a message from God, but instead of warring against principalities and powers, and the rulers of the darkness of the world, they form a hollow square, and turn the weapons of warfare against the church militant, be afraid of them. They do not bear the divine credentials. God has not given them any such burden of labor.[17]

No record tells what happened to Stanton after the 1893 crisis. Eugene Williams, the minister who initially sympathized with Stanton, moved to Michigan. He was replaced by William J. Stone, a seasoned minister who had been serving as the first president of the West Virginia Conference. At General Conference session, J. W. Watt requested a move closer to home. He had not brought his family from Missouri with him when he came to Montana in 1890. Probably because of the Stanton problem, the General Conference leaders convinced him to stay one more year in Montana.[18]

After the 1893 camp meeting in Livingston, Charles Martin held tent meetings in Billings, a town of 2,000 inhabitants along the Northern Pacific Railroad line. He organized a Sabbath school of seven members. Next, he took the tent to Miles City, another railroad town with a population of about 2,000. There he raised up a Sabbath school of 25 members. While Martin worked in the eastern portion of the state, Watt and Stone held tent meetings in Helena and organized a church of 13 members.[19]

In early 1894, Watt held meetings in the state's largest city, Butte City, a mining town of 30,000. A little later in the year, he accepted the presidency of the Indiana Conference. In a report to the *Review and Herald*, Watt stated: "When the writer entered the Montana Mission field four years ago, there were only about twenty-five Sabbath-keepers in the state. Now there are nearly 200."[20] Watt was replaced by J. R. Palmer, the president of the Colorado Conference.[21]

In 1895, Palmer and Stone held another series of meetings in Butte City and organized a church of 21 members.[22] Martin spent the early part of the year in Kalispell, where he organized a Sabbath school of 22 individuals.[23]

Later, Stone and C. E. Shafer held tent meetings in Great Falls. They organized a Sabbath school of 40 members and erected a church building.[24] Meanwhile, Martin conducted tent meetings in Missoula and organized a Sabbath school of 35 individuals.[25]

Palmer described the progress of the Montana Mission in a report to the *Review and Herald* in 1896 and he remarked on challenges of trying to evangelize such a large territory.

We now have companies quite well established at Helena, Butte, Bozeman, Livingston, Kalispell, Great Falls, Missoula, and Miles City. There are also other small Sabbath schools and scattered families in nearly all parts of the state. The Sabbath-keepers in the State now number two hundred and fifty.

Montana is a very large state. To make railroading practicable here, they have followed the crooked water courses. This makes the distance nearly a thousand miles from one end of the state to the other. The regular fare is from five to ten cents a mile. This makes expenses very high comparatively, especially where such great distances must be traveled to see so few people.[26]

The Montana Mission, with its 12 churches and 325 members, was organized into a conference in 1898. William Byington White, grandson of the first General Conference president, was elected as president of the conference having previously served as president of the Dakota, South Dakota, Nebraska, and Indiana conferences.[27]

Though the challenge of trying to reach a small population scattered over a large territory has continued to plague church leadership through the years, steady progress has been made in the Big Sky Country. Today nearly 40 churches and 3,350 members are spread across the wide-open spaces of Montana.[28]

18
The Story Uncle Arthur Got Wrong

For all those baby boomers (and all those before) who grew up as Seventh-day Adventist Christians, Uncle Arthur is a special person. He was the adult who wrote the exciting bedtime and Bible stories that provided them with hours of pleasure. They cannot forget the suspense in "Caught by the Tide" or the love in "The Stowaway" or the kindness in "Unlucky Jim." These stories caught their imagination and molded their thinking as they are still doing for children today.

Impossible as it may seem, there is however, one story Uncle Arthur got wrong. Now it was not entirely his fault, for he heard the story second hand. I discovered the real story while doing research in some old *Review and Heralds*.[1] Indeed, the real story is more amazing than Uncle Arthur's version ("The Flooded River").[2]

In 1894, the United States was in the midst of a terrible depression, the "Panic of 1893." In addition, the farmers in eastern Washington had just experienced crop failure. Times were really tough.[3] The Upper Columbia Conference camp meeting for that year was scheduled for May 30 to June 6 in the newly established town of College Place. The main speaker was a man who had been baptized in Walla Walla just 20 years earlier, had been given a license to preach, and had spent the next ten years establishing churches in the Northwest. Now he was coming back to his old stomping grounds. Despite tough times, every member wanted to hear Brother Alonzo T. Jones preach on righteousness by faith.

The winter just ended had experienced very heavy snowfalls in the mountains, so the rivers were running higher than anyone could remember. As a result, bridges had been swept away and train tracks washed out.

In May, the Adventists in the Palouse Hills of Washington began traveling toward College Place for camp meeting. When various groups arrived at the Snake River ferry, they discovered the water was too high for the ferry to run. The operator of the ferry considered the river unsafe. Before long, several Adventist groups were gathered at the ferry landing. Realizing they would miss camp meeting if the water did not subside, these believers knelt down and asked God to help them. As they prayed, the ferryman was on the other side of the river so there was no way for them to talk with him.

Soon several of the Adventist men saw a small boat on their side of the river. After some talking, they convinced the Indian who owned the boat to take one of them across the river to talk with the ferry operator.

When they reached the other side and talked with the ferryman, he would not budge. He insisted the river was unsafe. So the Indian began rowing the Adventist man back to his group. Part way across the river, they were surprised to see the ferry passing them. When the ferry operator arrived, he said to the Adventist groups, "You need not thank me, but thank your God; for the water has fallen two feet since I talked to the man you sent over."

After the Adventists were safely across the river, they again knelt to thank God for solving their problem in this miraculous way.[4]

19
Kellogg's Health System/Northwest

After several health-related visions and a visit to Jackson's health retreat, Ellen White called for the establishment of an Adventist health institute. Soon after the Civil War, the young Seventh-day Adventist Church of 4,000 members responded by starting the Western Health Reform Institute in Battle Creek, Michigan. For ten years the institute struggled, and at times it almost had to close. Then in 1876, John Harvey Kellogg, a young graduate from Bellevue Medical College, took over as medical superintendent. Under his leadership the institution made a dramatic turn around. By 1877 the institute erected a four-story building that was soon filled with patients. Other larger additions followed in 1884, 1887, 1889, and 1894.

By the turn of the century, the institute, renamed Battle Creek Sanitarium, had become one of the largest and most prominent health-related institutions in the United States. It employed more workers than the entire General Conference.[1] Its tremendous growth was a direct result of the blessings of God and the influence and genius of Dr. John Harvey Kellogg.

Kellogg was a much sought-after lecturer and speaker. He was the author of 50 books, a surgeon (22,000 surgeries performed), an aggressive health-reform advocate, teacher, administrator, and inventor. He is credited with having invented a number of breakfast cereals, peanut butter, a soybean milk substitute, several meat substitutes, a dynamometer to test muscle strength, several surgical instruments, the electric light cabinet bath, and the electric blanket.[2]

To many within the small Seventh-day Adventist denomination, Kellogg became a hero. They admired his genius and tried to emulate his success story by starting other health-related institutions. In 1893, the SDA Medical Missionary and Benevolent Association was launched to promote the establishment of Seventh-day Adventist medical institutions. Kellogg, who dominated this organization just as he did Battle Creek Sanitarium, called on the denomination's leaders to invest their meager funds in medical missionary institutions.[4] During 1893-1907, the Medical Association started several medical institutions in the Pacific Northwest. In late 1893, Dr. Kellogg encouraged his friend Dr. Lewis J. Belknap of Battle Creek to move to Portland, Oregon, and establish a small sanitarium.

On his trip to the Northwest, Belknap was robbed; later he lost his remaining possessions on a San Francisco dock. When he arrived in Portland, he had only five cents. With money borrowed from Thomas Starbuck, Belknap rented a house at Twelfth Street SE on the east side of the Willamette River. Here he opened a six-patient sanitarium.[5]

In 1894, the North Pacific Conference in session appointed a committee of five to take charge of the sanitarium. The committee's goal was to establish "in or near Portland, a health institution, to be conducted on the plan of the Sanitarium at Battle Creek and to be under its auspices."[6]

The next year, the successful sanitarium was moved across the Willamette River to the largest house in downtown Portland, the Reed Mansion. Here the sanitarium started a food factory and a school of nursing.

The Portland Sanitarium was moved again in 1902 to a three-acre site several miles east of town on the northwest slope of Mt. Tabor. A new sanitarium building was erected in the early 1920s at the Mt. Tabor site and the institution developed into a modern hospital.[7]

As the Battle Creek Sanitarium prospered, Kellogg began establishing a number of services for the poor of Chicago. These included a home for destitute and unwed mothers, a Helping Hand Mission for homeless men, dispensaries, an employment agency for released prisoners, a community health and recreation center for needy mothers and their children, and an evangelistic mission for the poor.[8]

Emulating Kellogg's activities, the Northwestern conferences established Helping Hand missions in Spokane, Butte, and Walla Walla in the late 1890s. These missions specialized in housing and feeding needy men for a minimal fee.[9] When, at the turn of the century, Ellen White warned the church against over-investing in humanitarian ministries, her advice, coupled with Kellogg's drift from the denomination, caused Adventists to lose interest in city missions.[10]

In 1893, Isaac Dunlap, the business manager of the newly established Walla Walla College, moved to Battle Creek to get medical training. He returned to College Place in 1899 and established treatment rooms in the basement of the college administration building.[11] The next year, the Upper Columbia Conference purchased the Francis Cook Mansion in Spokane and started the Mountain View Sanitarium.[12] When this sanitarium burned in 1904, the conference decided to take over Dunlap's privately owned sanitarium in College Place instead of rebuilding in Spokane.[13]

During this early period, the Walla Walla Sanitarium tried to benefit from the reputation of Dr. Kellogg's sanitarium. In Polk's 1905 *City Directory of Walla Walla*, the Walla Walla Sanitarium advertised itself as a branch of Battle Creek Sanitarium.[14] In those early days, patients could stay for only $12.50 per week. Quite a bargain compared to present-day hospital visits.

In 1907, the conference purchased the old College Place public school building and moved it to the present site of Walla Walla College library. The sanitarium was so successful that the building had to be enlarged three times.[15] Finally, the conference purchased a new hospital building on Bonsella Street in Walla Walla in 1931 and moved the sanitarium. Five years earlier, a group of physicians and businessmen had erected the structure but had been unsuccessful in their attempts to operate a hospital. At this new site, the Walla Walla Sanitarium became known as the Walla Walla General Hospital.[16] During its early years the Walla Walla Sanitarium, like the Portland Sanitarium, operated a food company. These food enterprises were simply attempts by Northwestern Adventists to duplicate Dr. Kellogg's success.[17]

During the years that Dr. Kellogg was breaking away from the denomination, a number of conference-owned as well as private Adventist-owned sanitariums were started in the Northwest: Seattle Sanitarium and Vegetarian Restaurant (1901), Tacoma Sanitarium

(1901), Whatcom (Bellingham) Sanitarium (1903), North Yakima Sanitarium (1905), Northwestern (Port Townsend) Sanitarium (1908), Boise Sanitarium (1908), Thornton's (Stevensville/Missoula, Montana) Sanitarium, Willamette (Salem) Sanitarium (1909), and Cottage Grove Sanitarium (1911).[19]

Most of these institutions flourished for a number of years, but by the end of the Great Depression in the late 1930s, all had been forced to close. Only two of the conference-owned institutions survived the Depression and continue as reminders of Kellogg's Health System/Northwest.

20
The Germans and Scandinavians

Today the Seventh-day Adventist Church works among a number of ethnic groups in the Northwest: Hispanics, Blacks, Native Americans, Koreans, Samoans, and Vietnamese. In the early days, the Adventist church directed its ethnic work primarily toward the Germans and Scandinavians. During the frontier days of the 1860s and 70s, the Chinese made up the Pacific Northwest's largest ethnic group. Most of them traveled to the untamed Wild West hoping to find work in railroad construction and mining.

Unfortunately, the rough and independent-minded pioneers of the region treated Oriental people with considerable disdain.[1] In 1885, the residents of Tacoma forced 7,000 Chinese residents, 10 percent of the city's population, to leave town. Similar expulsions took place at many locations throughout western Washington Territory.[2] Two years later, a group of cowboys raided a Chinese mining camp in Hells Canyon in eastern Oregon. Unable to find the Chinese cache of gold, the cowboys tortured and finally shot to death the 31 miners.[3]

In 1894, the Adventist Church in Portland tried to reach the Chinese and Japanese by operating a small school for them. This school was discontinued after several years, probably because of the declining Chinese population.[4]

By 1890, the Germans and Scandinavians were the two largest ethnic groups in the Northwest. Immigrants from the Scandinavian countries came to the Puget Sound because of its similarity to their homeland, while the Germans were drawn to the rich farmland of the Palouse Hills in eastern Washington.[5]

As early as 1861, a small group of Scandinavians in southern

Wisconsin joined the newly formed Seventh-day Adventist Church and organized the first ethnic congregation in the denomination. Two years later, John Matteson, a Baptist minister who had come to Wisconsin from Denmark, accepted the Adventist message along with most of his congregation. Before long, Matteson began traveling to groups of Scandinavian immigrants throughout the Midwest, raising up Adventist churches.[6] By 1877, 800 Scandinavians in North America had become Seventh-day Adventists.[7] A few of these Scandinavian Adventists moved to the Pacific Northwest in the 1800s.[8]

Two Scandinavian families who had accepted Adventism in Minnesota moved to Monitor, Oregon, in 1890. They established a small Adventist church of seven members. By 1900, this church with a membership of 67 had become the largest Scandinavian Adventist church on the West Coast.[9]

The first attempt by Northwestern Adventists to work for the Scandinavian population of the region seems to have been in the Upper Columbia Conference. In the early 1890s, this conference sent Albert G. Christiansen, a Danish student who had learned to read and write English at Milton Academy, to Union College in Nebraska to study in the Scandinavian Department.[10] When he returned in 1894, he began holding evangelistic meetings among his people.[11]

By the turn of the century, several ministers were working in both the North Pacific and Upper Columbia Conferences among the Scandinavians. Through their efforts, Scandinavian churches were established at many locations throughout the Northwest, some of which are still in operation today, although services are held in English.[12]

German immigrants in the Midwest began accepting the Adventist message in 1870. One of these was Louis Conradi who attended Battle Creek College and finished the four-year course in a little over a year. In 1881 Conradi began holding evangelistic meetings for the German immigrants of the Midwest. The next year he was joined by Henry Shultz, another German who had been serving as the president of the Nebraska Conference.[13]

By 1889, the German work in North America had grown to 1,300 members, including twenty churches and six ministers.[14] Frederick Jorg, one of these ministers, transferred from Nebraska to the

North Pacific Conference to start the German work in the western portions of Oregon and Washington. His efforts met with such success that two years later Gottfried F. Haffner was sent from Kansas to assist him.[15]

In 1890 and 1891, Shultz, now director of the German work in North America, attended the camp meetings in the Upper Columbia Conference. He preached for the 20 to 30 Germans who attended.[16] Following camp meeting, he traveled to Farmington, Washington, and organized a small German church.[17] In 1892, Haffner transferred to the Upper Columbia Conference.[18] In March 1893, he reported to the *Review and Herald*: "In Walla Walla I baptized seventeen, in Farmington eighteen, in Spokane nine, and in Ritzville two."[19] The same year Haffner started a German church of 40 members in Walla Walla; this church later moved to College Place. In 1911, they erected a church on the northwest corner of Sixth Street SW and Bade Avenue SW. This German church, which had a membership of 97 in 1942, continued to operate until 1955.[20] In 1893 Haffner also visited a colony of Germans along the Palouse River where he baptized members of the Ochs, Schierman, and Weitz families and established the Endicott church.[21] My great-grandparents, Phillip and Katherine Rudy, joined this church in 1911. They were Germans who had been living along the Volga River in Russia. The night before they left for America, Katherine had a dream about two men preaching about the Sabbath. Even though all her family were Lutherans, Katherine was impressed that they should join the church of the two men when they arrived in America. It was a little over four years later that the Rudys were invited to a series of religious meetings at Conrad Schierman's home along the Palouse River. When Katherine entered the home, she could not believe her eyes: the men scheduled to speak (Gottfried F. Haffner and Jacob Riffel) were the same men of her dream. At the end of the meetings, the ministers baptized the Rudys in the Palouse River through a hole cut into the ice.[22] Several years later, the Rudys purchased a farm west of Colfax. Here they attended the Wilcox German Church.[23]

By 1906, nine German churches with a membership of about 200 had been established in the Upper Columbia Conference. A few other German churches were established in the Northwest conferences.[24]

From 1900 to 1930, the Adventist message spread rapidly among the Germans in America. By 1925, over 100 German-speaking churches were west of the Mississippi River with a total membership of around 4,000; east of the Mississippi only 17 churches were organized with a membership of 900.[25]

Although today the Seventh-day Adventist Church is directing its ethnic work toward different groups, its goal is still the same—to preach the everlasting gospel "to every nation, tribe, tongue, and people" (Revelation 14:6, NKJV).

21
Evangelism in the Wild West

When the transcontinental railroads arrived in the 1880s, the Northwest was finally connected to the rest of the United States with a rapid and safe form of transportation. Settlers moved in and homesteaded the land at an incredible rate. The population of Washington Territory skyrocketed from 75,116 in 1880 to 357,232 by 1890. The territories of Idaho and Montana saw a fourfold jump in their population during this period; and Oregon experienced a more modest increase of 100 percent.[1]

While the Northwest was being tamed by the plow, the Adventists were establishing churches. During its first 18 years in the region made up of Idaho, Montana, Oregon, and Washington, the denomination raised up 57 congregations. Adventist ministers were not assigned to specific churches as they are today. They traveled from town to town conducting evangelistic meetings in large halls or tents. Their mission was to start congregations in the various towns and cities of their conference territory.

Because of this focus, the ministry placed little emphasis on nurturing existing churches. As a result, many newly established churches died. Of the 57 churches started in the Pacific Northwest during the first 18 years, 26 of them—almost half—were closed by the turn of the century.[2] In spite of this weakness, Northwestern Adventism in the 1800s grew at a respectable rate. From 1875 to 1900, denominational presence in the region increased from one congregation of 100 members to 114 churches of 4,284 members. But this growth did not come easy.[3]

In 1896, C. N. Martin was sent to Stevensville, Montana, to raise up an Adventist group. He described the difficulties in a report to the *Review and Herald*: "I came to this place about the first of April. Every Seventh-day Adventist preacher can understand my feelings and situation on my arrival. I was without friend, no home was open to me but the hotel at two dollars a day, and I had an unpopular truth to present."[4]

Pioneering preachers had to contend with strong opposition and, at times, even persecution as they entered these unworked areas. The experience of D. E. Scoles in Joseph, Oregon, a remote corner of the Wild West, is an example of this. In 1892, the only church building in this rough cattle town was the Presbyterian church. It had been erected by the people of Joseph to be "open to all orthodox denominations." Since the Adventist Church was considered an "orthodox denomination," Scoles was given permission to use the structure. Part way through his lectures, he began speaking on the Sabbath issue. This upset the Presbyterian minister so much he circulated a petition to force Scoles out of the building.

Describing his experience in a report for the *Review and Herald*, Scoles wrote:

> But one of our brethren owned a building on Main Street, so we seated it and arranged for meetings. The next morning after we began, the whole front of the building was painted with vulgar and threatening notices, and I was hung in effigy in the street. But we thought there must be some grain among the weeds, or Satan would not be so angry, hence we continued, but things went from bad to worse. They smashed windows, threw cayenne pepper over the stove and on the floor, in the meantime threatening to "egg" me out of town, and give me a coat of "tar and feathers."

During the final meeting of the series the mob yelled, stomped, threw rocks on the roof, and tossed lighted firecrackers into the building. The harassment became so intense that Scoles finally closed the meeting. In his final report to the *Review and Herald*, he wrote:

> The town authorities were appealed to for protection, but would do nothing; however, no personal violence was done. . . . Seven have

decided to keep all of God's commandments; two of the wealthiest and most influential ladies of the town are among the number.[5]

Reports sent into the *Review and Herald* during these early days were often filled with accounts of persecution. In fact, pioneering preachers counted on it when they entered unworked areas.

In 1897, C. T. Shafer conducted a series of meetings in the isolated town of Elkhorn, Montana. He was continually bothered by the children, whom he described as wicked. They threw rocks at his tent, made noise to disturb his meetings, tossed firecrackers, and "whipped the canvas." Though frustrated with the youths' behavior, Shafer remained calm. He wrote: "We have here an excellent opportunity for the love of God to shine forth. Perhaps it may win some soul from among these youth to Him."[6]

Usually, however, the opposition originated from ministers of other denominations. In 1891, J. E. Fulton and R. D. Benham held evangelistic meetings in Cottage Grove, Oregon. The Methodist minister was so upset with them that he preached a sermon on the Seventh-day Adventist Church. In his *Review and Herald* report, Benham wrote:

> The sermon was filled with bitter invectives and vituperations, mingled with abundant false statements. He called us "modern Pharisees, Saturday idolaters, children of the Devil,' etc., and said that 'the poison of asps was under our tongues." [7]

A similar experience happened to J. W. Watt and E. R. Williams in the rough mining town of Virginia City, Montana, in 1890. In his report Watt wrote:

> In his sermon [against Adventists], Elder Mills [a circuit-riding Methodist minister] ran over about the same line of Scriptures that is usually brought forward to prove first-day sacredness. . . . He classed us with saloon-keepers, gamblers, infidels, blacklegs, and all kinds of irreligious persons, and remarked that a man is known by the company he keeps.[8]

At other times the ministers of the town would attack the

Adventist preacher through the local newspaper. In 1893, D. E. Scoles traveled to the small farming town of Athena in eastern Oregon and erected his tent near the Baptist church. According to *Athena Press*, the weekly newspaper, Scoles attracted "large crowds every evening."[9]

The two ministers in town became furious and used their worship services as opportunities to combat the Adventist teachings, but Scoles continued to draw large crowds. Frustrated, J. B. Daisley, the pastor of the Christian Church, sent a letter to the newspaper accusing Scoles of teaching false doctrines.[10] The next week Scoles sent his response to the newspaper, showing how his teachings came from the Bible.[11] This made Daisley so irate that he responded by placing a long, two-column article against Scoles in the next issue, employing some pretty strong language against the Adventist minister.[12]

Scoles, not wanting to be outdone, attacked the teachings of Daisley's church. Unfortunately, he, too, used some strong words. He wrote: "Elder Daisley seems to take my last article very hard: but it is no wonder when we remember that, 'It is the shot bird that flutters.'" At another place he referred to Daisley as a man whose "mind [is] dwarfed by the soul destroying doctrines of antinomianism."[13]

In the next issue of the *Athena Press*, Daisley took up two columns on the front page to put down Scoles. His article appeared next to one about the Chicago World's Fair. He began by alluding to Scoles' bird illustration.

> Our Advent friend reminds me of the Irishman who was telling a neighbor how he shot a bird. . . . He said, "The first toime I shot im, I missed im; and the sekond toime I shot im, I hit him roight whare I missed im before."[14]

Though Scoles' next response never reached the front page of the paper, it was published.[15] The following week, Daisley ended the newspaper debate with the words, "Can anything be more utterly baseless—more flatly in contradiction to all Bible teaching than 7th dayism."[16]

From our comfortable standpoint, it is easy to point out the mistakes and criticize the unrefined methods of our pioneering ministers and laity. But, though they had their faults, we cannot help but be impressed by their dedication and sacrifice. Their task of dispersing Adventism to the unworked towns and cities of the Wild West was not an easy one.

22
Frontier Religion

Though Sabbatarian Adventism was born in the well-established region of New England, the leaders of the movement soon discovered that the greatest potential for growth was on the western frontier. With this new understanding, they shifted their evangelistic efforts to the frontier and semi-frontier states of the Upper Lakes (Michigan and Wisconsin), and the North Central (west of the Mississippi River), Rocky Mountain, and West Coast regions, and success followed.

By 1875 and continuing through 1900, two-thirds of the total membership of the denomination resided in states that had been first entered by Adventist ministers within 20 years of statehood. By 1885, these states also contained the six largest conferences.[1] Though these states held most of the church membership, they accounted for only 23% of the nation's population.[2]

During its formative years (1860s-1900), Adventism emerged as a frontier religion. Transferring their headquarters and publishing house to the semi-frontier state of Michigan in 1855, the young movement began to shift its emphasis from New England to the Midwest. This westward shift continued in 1874 with the launching of its second publishing house in Oakland, California.

As a frontier religion, one would expect Adventism to have good success in the remote frontier of the Pacific Northwest, and this is exactly what happened. By 1900, membership in the Northwest stood at 4,284 members. This was with a member to nonmember ratio, 1 to 311, four times lower than the national average for the Seventh-day Adventist Church.[3]

Adventism's amazing growth in the Northwest can be attributed partially to the fact that the denomination entered this region when it was a lightly populated frontier. When Isaac Van Horn began his evangelistic meetings in Walla Walla in 1874, the population of Washington Territory was only 50,000. J. J. Smith found a similar population as he entered Idaho Territory in 1884. Adventist ministers to Oregon and Montana Territory found somewhat larger populations on their arrival. Undoubtedly, one of the greatest keys to the Adventist success in the Northwest was its early entrance into the region. This gave the denomination an advantage that it enjoyed in only a few other locations.[4]

Over the years, Northwest Adventism has changed dramatically. No longer do we conduct evangelistic meetings in canvas tents, travel on Columbia River steamboats, or operate small sanitariums. The frontier days are gone forever, but the special message these pioneering ministers brought to the remote Pacific Northwest over 100 years ago has not changed. Adventists in the Northwest still cling to it and still hope for Jesus' soon return.

Stephen Maxson

Lois Maxson

Caroline Wood

James Franklin Wood

Isaac D. Van Horn was the first SDA minister to work in the Pacific Northwest.

In 1874, Alonzo T. Jones was baptized by Van Horn in Walla Walla and entered the ministry, serving in the Northwest for 10 years.

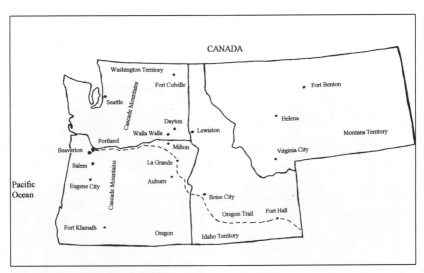

The Pacific Northwest in 1873

The Walla Walla SDA Church building, erected in 1875, was the first Seventh-day Adventist church structure in the Northwest.

The Milton SDA church building was erected in 1877.

Alonzo T. Jones built the Farmington SDA Church in Washington Territory "with my own hands" in 1883.

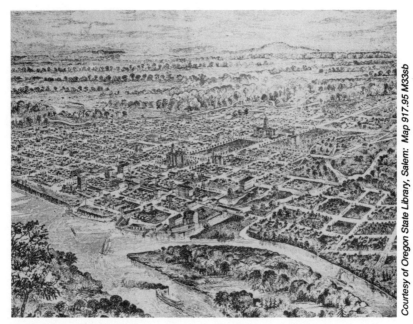

In 1876, Adventists held evangelistic meetings at Marion Square, between Front and Commercial Streets, and Marion and Union Streets, and organized a church. This bird's-eye lithograph of Salem was produced in 1876.

George and Helen Conard

In 1877, Thomas H. Starbuck was baptized by Van Horn in Salem. He later served the Adventist church as minister and educator.

Courtesy of Walla Walla College Library

William Nichols was an early member of the Adventist church in the Walla Walla Valley.

Courtesy of Walla Walla College Library

George Colcord served as the first president of the Upper Columbia Conference.

Courtesy of the Walla Walla College Library

In 1892, the Upper Columbia Conference built a tract and missionary store. In 1897, William Nichols purchased it and his son operated a dry goods and grocery store here for many years. Today it is known as the College Store.

Courtesy of Walla Walla College Library

O. A. Johnson was the first SDA minister to hold evangelistic meetings in Montana Territory.

137

Clarence and Minnie Ford served in the Upper Columbia Conference for many years.

Ninevah Ford came west with Dr. Marcus Whitman in 1843.

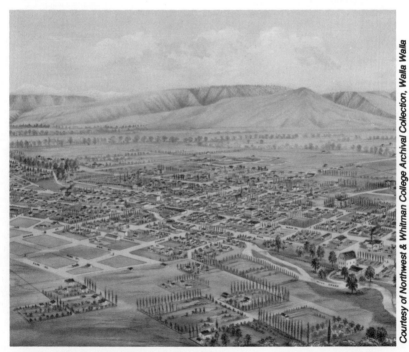

In 1874, Isaac D. Van Horn held evangelistic tent meetings in Walla Walla and organized a church. The next year the believers erected a church building at the corner of Fourth and Birch Streets. This bird's-eye lithograph of Walla Walla was produced in 1876. Notice the SDA church.

During the 1800s, Ellen White made three visits to the Northwest.

During the 1800s, John Loughborough made several visits to the Northwest from California.

A North Pacific Conference camp meeting held at the turn of the century. The location is unknown.

Isaac Van Horn and Alonzo Jones held tent meetings in Portland in 1877 with minimal results. In 1882 Charles Boyd was able to organize a church in Portland. This bird's-eye lithograph was produced in 1881.

The Pacific Northwest in 1884

During the 1880s, the North Pacific Academy operated in Portland, Oregon.

During the 1880s, the Milton Academy operated in Milton, Oregon.

Charles Boyd held tent meetings in Seattle and organized a church in 1886. This lithograph of Seattle was produced in 1884.

Daniel T. and L.A. Fero worked in all three Northwestern conferences in the late 1800s.

Charles Boyd served as the second president of the North Pacific Conference.

Courtesy of Loma Linda University

Courtesy of Walla Walla College Library

Henry Decker served as president of the Upper Columbia Conference and later as president of the North Pacific Conference.

Edward Sutherland served as the first president of Walla Walla College.

Courtesy of Historical Photograph Collections, Washington State University Libraries: #89-027

Henry Decker and Clarence Ford held tent meetings in Spokane Falls in 1886 and organized a church for this town in 1888. This bird's-eye lithograph of Spokane Falls was produced in 1884.

Walla Walla College Administration Building (left) and the Walla Walla
Sanitarium (right) in the early 1900s.

This church building on the campus of Walla Walla College was completed in
1920. It is known today as Village Hall.

Mount Ellis Academy near Bozeman, Montana, at the time of the 1926 Montana Conference camp meeting.

The Portland Sanitarium in 1903

In the 1880s, J. J. Smith and then Daniel T. Fero conducted evangelistic meetings in Boise City in Idaho Territory. In 1886, Fero was able to organize a church in this town. This bird's-eye lithograph of Boise City was produced in 1890.

Ministers at the Washington Conference camp meeting in Kent, Washington, in 1907. From left to right on the front row: E. L. Stewart, Boynton, Henry W. Decker, A. J. Breed, Lewis Johnson, W. W. Sharp. Second row: H.C.J. Wollekar, F. M. Burg, George Enoch, O.E. Davis, A. J. Stone. Back row: Stiles, C. E. Weeks, Russell, J. A. Holbrook, J. J. Clark, Verts, Johnson, unknown.

146

Ministers at the North Pacific Conference camp meeting in Portland in 1890. From left to right on the front row: J. C. Bunch, R.D. Benham, John M. Cole, Volney H. Lucas, W.C. Ward, William Potter, H.W. Babcock, and John Graham. Center row: Isaac Morrison, unknown. Back row: Thomas H. Starbuck, Obed Dickinson, W.W. Sharp, H.W. Reed, Elder R. A. Underwood, Daniel T. Jones, Henry W. Decker, H. Shultz, and Fried Jorg.

1913 Washington Conference camp meeting in Auburn, Washington

Courtesy of the Washington Conference of SDA

Northwestern Sanitarium in Port Townsend, Washington, in 1907

Courtesy of Arlene Johnson

My great grandparents, Phillip and Katherine Rudy, joined the German-speaking Wilcox SDA church near Colfax, Washington, in the early 1900s.

Courtesy of the Idaho Conference of SDA

In 1882, Will W. Steward learned of Adventism from Alonzo Jones in Farmington, Washington Territory. He served many years as a minister in the Upper Columbia Conference and as the first president of the Idaho Conference.

148

References

Space limitations have dictated that the references be as brief as possible. To accomplish this goal, abbreviations for some names, institutions and publications have been used. Nonetheless, those who want to check an interpretation or extend the research will find sufficient information.

EGW	Ellen G. White
JSW	James S. White
MS	*Manuscript*
RH	*Review and Herald*
SDA Ency	*Seventh-day Adventist Encyclopedia*
SDA Y	*Seventh-day Adventist Yearbook*
ST	*Signs of the Times*
TI	*Testimonies for the Church*
WCW	Willie C. White

Endnotes

1 The Northwest's First Adventist

[1]Alvin M. Josephy, *Nez Perce Country: National Park Handbook* (Washington, DC: National Park Service, 1983), 45-50.

[2]Ibid., 63-75.

[3]Ibid., 92-96.

[4]*RH*, 19 November 1903, 28; Mildred Searcey, *We Remember* (Pendleton, OR: Eastern Oregon Pub. Co, 1973), 92; *East Oregonian Anniversary Edition* (newspaper), 26 October 1955, 2.

[5]Seventh-day Adventist Encyclopedia (Washington, DC: Review and Herald Publishing Assoc., 1966), 605 (hereafter SDAEncy).

[6]*RH*, 19 November 1903, 28.

[7]*SDAEncy* 605.

[8]*East Oregonian Anniversary Edition*, 26 October 1955, 2; Frank T. Gilbert, *Historical Sketches of Walla Walla, Whitman, Columbia and Garfied Counties* (Portland, OR: A. G. Walling, 1882), appendix, 62.

[9]*Deed Book* C, 26 Pendleton, OR: Umatilla County Clerk Office, 11 June 1877), 436.

[10]Bob Grant, "Early Photographer Leaves 10,000 Plates," *Pioneer Trails* (Pendleton, OR: Umatilla County Historical Society, April 1979), 4; Josephy, 97-102.

[11]Lee Moorhouse, *Souvenir Album of Noted Indian Photographs* (Pendleton, OR: East Oregonian Print, 1906).

[12]Searcey, 92-99.

[13]*RH*, 28 April 1868, 315.

[14]*Deed Book H*, (Pendleton, OR: Umatilla County Clerk Office, April 1882), 210.

2 He Couldn't Hide from the Sabbath

[1]*RH*, 20 November 1879, 168; H. K. Hines, *An Illustrated History of the State of Washington* (Chicago: Lewis Pub. Co., 1893), 416.

[2]W. D. Lyman, *An Illustrated History of Walla Walla County* (n.p.: W.H. Lever Pub., 1901), 485; Minnie Ford, *"Some Early History"* (handwritten account of the early history of the Maxson family and the Upper Columbia

Conference of SDA by James F. Wood's daughter), 1.; James F. Wood, "Medical Lake Ledger", 15 July 1892. (newspaper article account of his trip over the Oregon Trail.)

[3]Frances Maxson Brincherhoff, "Remembrances of a Pioneer" (typed two-page account of the Maxson's trip over the Oregon Trail by Stephen Maxson's daughter) n.d.

[4] *Sixty Years of Progress: The Anniversary History of Walla Walla* (College Place, WA.: College Press, 1952), 56.

[5]Brincherhoff, 2.

[6]*Deed Book K*, (Walla Walla, WA: Walla Walla Country Clerk Office, 28 September 1872), 54.

[7]Gilbert, 229, 385-386.

[8]*Sixty Years*, 60-61.

[9]Dan Shultz, *A Great Tradition*, (College Place, WA.: Color Press, 1992), 14.

[10]*RH*, 17 June 1873, 6; Doug R. Johnson, *Adventism in the Pacific Northwest* (Olympia, WA: American Speedy Printing, 1989), 2-3; Ford, 3-4; Rufus Wood to Edith, 26 April 1929.

[11]*SDAEncy*, 187; Harold McCumber, *Pioneering the Message in the Golden West* (Mountain View, CA: Pacific Press Pub. Assoc., 1946), 80-81.

[12]*RH*, 17 June 1873, 6; Ford, with author; 3-5; *RH*, 9 November 1869, 157.

[13]Caroline Eros written interview with author, January 1992; *RH*, 9 November 1869, 157; Church Record Book (Walla Walla City SDA Church) 17 May 1874, 1.

[14]*RH*, 9 November 1869, 157; *RH*, 17 June 1873, 6; Ford, 3-4.

[15]Dennis Casper interview by author, 1992; Rufus Wood to Edith, 26 April 1929; *RH*, 17 June 1873, 6; *RH*, 3 November 1977, 4.

[16]*North Pacific Union Gleaner*, 3 June 1930, 9; 21 July 1921, 1.

[17]Ford, 5.

[18]*RH*, 17 June 1873, 6.

[19]*RH*, 22 July 1873, 46; *RH*, 26 August 1873, 87; Randal F. Barlow, "Work in the North Pacific Union from Conception through Birth—1878" paper for Andrews University class, 1977), 9-10.

3 A Missionary for the Northwest

[1]*RH*, 6 October 1910, 9; *SDAEncy*, 434, 1372.

[2]*RH*, 7 April 1874, 134; Harold McCumber, *The Advent Message in the Golden West* (Mountain View, CA: Pacific Press Pub. Assoc., 1968), 86.

[3]*RH*, 28 April 1874, 160; *RH*, 9 June 1874, 207.

[4]Ford, 5; Barlow, 13; *RH*, 29 August 1940, 26.

[5]Adelia P. Van Horn to JSW & EGW, 20 April 1874.

[6]Rufus Wood to Edith, 26 April 1929; *History of the Walla Walla City SDA Church* (Walla Walla, WA: City Church, 1974) a centennial booklet; Gilbert, 308, 314.

[7]Rufus Wood to Edith, 26 April 1929.

[8]*RH*, 9 June 1874, 207.

[9]Church Record Book, May 17, 1874, 1-2.

[10]*RH*, 25 August 1874, 78.

[11]*RH*, 26 August 1875, 62.

[12]Alonzo T. Jones to Commissioners of Pension, May 10, 1916; Keith A. Murray, *The Modocs and Their War* (Norman, OK: 1959), 180-222; George W. Fuller, *A History of the Pacific Northwest* (New York,: Alfred A. Knopf, 1931), 262- 264.

[13]*ST*, 25 June 1874, 24; *ST*, 9 July 1874, 32; *ST*, 23 July 1874, 40; *RH*, 25 August 1874, 78.

[14]*ST*, 25 June 1874, 24.

[15]*Walla Walla Union*, 25 April 1874, 3; *ST*, 17 September 1874, 55; *ST*, 4 March 1875, 136; *ST*, 27 May 1875, 230.

[16]Gilbert, 327-331; *RH*, 5 August 1875, 46.

[17]*ST*, 4 March 1875, 136.

[18]*ST*, 17 September 1874, 55; *RH*, 3 November 1874, 149; *Gleaner*, 15 June 1916, 8; *ST*, 11 March 1875, 142.

[19]*ST*, 11 March 1875, 142; *RH*, 24 June 1875, 262.

[20]*RH*, 22 April 1875, 132; *ST*, 27 May 1875, 230; *RH*, 24 June 1875, 262; *ST*, 26 August 1875, 334; *RH*, 29 August 1940, 26.

[21]*RH*, 26 August 1875, 62.

[22]*ST*, 8 June 1876, 208.

4 The Upper Country

[1]*RH*, 26 August 1875, 62; *ST*, 2 November 1876, 360.

[2]*ST*, 16 November 1877, p 351; *RH*, 10 July 1879, 23; James F. Wood's 1879 Ministerial License.

[3]Gilbert, appendix, 61; *Deed Book B* (Portland, OR: Umatilla County Clerk Office, 5 June 1871), Church Record Book, 3.

[4]*ST*, 3 May 1877, 144.

[5]*ST*, 26 April 1877, 133.

[6]*Pacific Union Recorder*, 17 January 1907.

[7]*ST*, 11 October 1877, 312; *ST*, 15 November 1877, 350-351.

[8]*ST*, 29 November 1877, 368; Gilbert (a line drawing of the Milton SDA Church with the caption, "Seventh-day Adventist, Milton, OR, Erected 1877"); *Dayton SDA Church, 1876-1987* (church history booklet);n.p.; *RH*, 22 April 1880, 268.

[9]*ST*, 12 September 1878; *Sixty Years*, 75; Caroline Eros written interview by author, January, 1992.

[10]*RH*, 20 November 1879, 168.

[11]Shultz, *A Great Tradition*, 15; Caroline Eros written interview by author, January 1992.

[12]Church Record Book, minutes of the meeting 15 March 1883, 13, 14; 4 January 1885, 18, 19.

[13]*RH*, 5 May 1885, 283.

[14]Ford, 9; *RH*, 3 July 1888, 428.

[15]James F. Wood to Caroline Wood and children, 7 December 1894.

[16]Gilbert, 316-317; *ST*, 12 September 1878; *ST*, 5 December 1878; *RH*, 10 July 1879, 23.

[17]*ST*, 5 December 1878.

[18]*RH*, 26 June 1879, 5; *Walla Walla Union*, 24 June 1879; *RH*, 10 July 1879, 21.

[19]*RH*, 19 July 1879, 23.

[20]EGW to JSW, 20 May 1880.

[21]*RH*, 15 July 1880, 61; *RH*, 17 June 1880, 394; *RH*, 28 October 1880, 280.

[22]Ford, 5; *RH*, 25 November 1902, 23; *RH*, 8 July 1880, 41.

5 The Willamette Valley

[1]*RH*, 29 June 1876, 6; *RH*, 31 August 1876, 78.

[2]*ST*, 10 August 1876; *RH*, 13 August 1876, 78; *RH*, 21 September 1876, 102; Lancaster Pollard, *Oregon and the Pacific Northwest* (Portland, OR: Binfords & Mort Pub.), 203.

[3]Edith Starbuck, The Early Story of the Oregon Conference (typed, 56-page history by Thomas Starbuck's daughter, 1930), 6; *Gleaner*, 2 September 1930, 14.

[4]Starbuck, 6-8; Ella M. Robinson, *Lighter of Gospel Fires* (Mountain View, CA.: Pacific Press Pub. Assoc., 1954), 131, 132; *Sixty Years*, 19; Sylvia Zitek, *Except As We Forget* (Gresham, OR: Three Cedars Pub. Assn., 1978), 16-18.

[5]*RH*, 21 September 1876, 102.

[6]Starbuck, 9-15; *ST*, 25 January 1877; *ST*, 22 March 1877, 104; *ST*, 31

May 1877.

[7]*RH*, 11 September 1930, 29.

[8]*RH*, 3 January 1893, 15; H.O. Lang, *History of the Willamette Valley* (n.p., 1885); 803; Starbuck, 16.

[9]*Daily Stateman* (quoted by *RH*, 3 January 1893, 15).

[10]Lang, 803; *RH*, 3 January 1893, 15.

[11]Starbuck, 11-12.

[12]Ibid.; *RH*, 26 July 1881, 76.

[13]*General Conference Bulletin*,8 March 1891, 26.

[14]*ST*, 16 November 1876; *ST*, 15 February 1877, 64.

[15]*ST*, 31 May 1877.

[16]Isaac D. Van Horn to JSW, 16 April 1877.

[17]Ibid; idem to EGW, 1 April 1884.

[18]George R. Knight, *From 1888 to Apostasy* (Washington, D C: Review and Herald Pub. Assoc., 1987), 18.

[19]I. Van Horn to EGW, 1 April 1884.

[20]APVH to JSW, 26 August 1877.

[21]Ibid; idem JSW, 5 August 1877.

[22]IDVH to JSW, 5 September 1877.

[23]Carlos Schwantes, *The Pacific Northwest: An Interpretive History* (Lincoln, NE: University of Nebraska Press, 1989), 194-195.

[24]*ST*, 6 September 1877, 280; *ST*, 4 October 1877, 304; Starbuck, 32; *The Daily Oregonian*, 13 July 1877; *RH*, 21 June 1877, 198; A. Van Horn to JSW, 26 August 1877; Schwantes, *Gleaner*, 192.

[25]Starbuck, 21-24; *Gleaner*, 5 January 1937, 7; *SDA Yearbook*, 1906, 63; *SDA Yearbook, 1910*, 64; A. Van Horn to JSW, 26 August 1877.

[26]*ST*, 18 July 1878, 216; *RH*, 15 August 1878, 63; *RH*, 1 August 1878, 47; EGW, Letter 40, 1878.

[27]I. Van Horn to EGW, 1 April 1884.

[28]EGW to Isaac and Adelia Van Horn, Letter 51a, 1878.

[29]I. Van Horn to EGW, 1 April 1884.

[30]EGW to JSW, 16 May 1880.

[31]EGW to JSW, 20 May 1880.

[32]I. Van Horn to EGW, 4 August 1880.

[33]*ST*, 12 September 1878; *RH*, 21 November 1878, 166; *RH*, 10 July 1879, 23; *RH*, 27 March 1879, 102; Starbuck, 22-24.

[34]*ST*, 12 September 1878; *ST*, 5 December 1878.

[35]*RH*, 26 June 1879, 5; *RH*, 17 July 1879, 28; *RH*, 20 November 1879, 166.

[36]I. Van Horn to EGW, 4 August 1880.

[37]*ST*, 15 July 1880, 321; I. Van Horn to EGW, 4 August 1880.

[38]*RH*, 6 October 1910, 9.

[39]M. Ellsworth Olsen, *HOPSA*, (Washington, DC: Review and Herald Pub. Assoc., 1925), 319-320.

[40]*RH*, 6 October 1910, 9.

[41]EGW to I. Van Horn, 20 January 1893.

[42]I. Van Horn to EGW, 9 March 1893.

[43]Arthur Spalding, *Captains of the Host* (Washington, DC: Review and Herald Pub. Assoc., 1949), 205.

6 Ellen White Visits the Northwestern Frontier

[1]Arthur L. White, *Ellen G. White: The Lonely Years* (Washington, DC.: Review and Herald Pub. Assoc., 1984), 36-48.

[2]*ST*, 25 April 1878, 128; *ST*, 2 May 1878, 136.

[3]Schwantes, 155; *RH*, July 18, 1878, 31; EGW, I 4:286-290.

[4]*ST*, 18 July 1878.

[5]EGW, MS 4, 1878, 1, (EGW, *Manuscript Releases*, Vol. 5, 178).

[6]*ST*, 25 July 1878.

[7]*RH*, 18 July 1878, 31.

[8]*ST*, 1 August 1878; EGW to JSW, Letter 32, 1878.

[9]EGW, I 4, 291.

[10]*RH*, 1 August 1878, 47.

[11]*ST*, 18 July 1878, 216; *RH*, 10 July 1879, 21.

[12]Arthur L. White, *The Lonely Years*, 88.

[13]EGW, T4: 295; EGW to JSW, 11 July 1878, 2-3.

[14]EGW to JSW, 11 July 1878, 2-3.

[15]*ST*, 22 April 1880, 189; *ST*, 13 May 1880.

[16]*RH*, 17 June 1880, 394; *RH*, 15 July 1880, 61; *ST*, 17 June 1880.

[17]EGW to JSW, 16 May 1880.

[18]EGW, TS: 285-287; Doug R. Johnson, "Information Concerning Testimonies for the Church, Volume Five, Pages 249-302" (a five-page unpublished paper).

[19]EGW to JSW, 20 May 1880.

[20]*ST*, 15 November 1877, 349, 351; EGW, MS 11, 1891 (EGW, *Sermon and Talks*, 166).

[21]EGW, 283; EGW to JSW, 20 May 1880.

[22]EGW, MS 11, 1891, 166-168.

[23]EGW to JSW, 20 May 1880.

[24]Ibid.; *RH*, 17 June 1880, 394.

[25]*ST*, 24 June 1880, 284.

[26]EGW to JSW, 23 June 1880.

[27]Starbuck, 15.

[28]EGW to JSW, 23 June 1880.

[29]EGW to Edson and Emma White, 14 June 1880.

7 William Nichols

[1]Richard L. Rieck, "A Geography of Death on the Oregon-California Trail, 1840-1860," *Overland Journal* 9, no. 1, 1991, 13-21.

[2]Journal of William H. Babcock, 1859 (Whitman College Library, Walla Walla, WA.).

[3]Gilbert, appendix, 28; *Gleaner*, 3 June 1930, 9.

[4]Merrill J. Mattes, *Platte River Road Narrative* (Chicago, Ill.: University of Illinois Press), 1-5, 542-555.

[5]Gilbert, appendix 28.

[6]*Gleaner*, 3 June 1930, 9; *The History of Klamath Country Oregon*, (Portland, OR: Taylor Pub. Co., 1984), 18.

[7]*RH*, 19 July 1864, 63.

[8]*SDAEncy*, 187; Ella M. Robinson, 131-133.

[9]*Sixty Years*, 62.

[10]1885 R.L. Inland Empire Directory.

[11]Gilbert, 28; Jonathan Edwards, *An Illustrated History of Spokane County*, (n.p.: W. H. Lever, 1900), 268-270.

[12]*Early History of the Milton-Freewater Area*, 13-14; Robert S. Folkenberg to author, 19 February 1992.

[13]*Gleaner*, 16 July 1925, 8-9; *Milton Eagle*, 30 December 1937; *Milton Eagle*, 22 May 1924.

[14]*Milton Eagle*, 1937.

[15]*Sixty Years*, 71; *Gleaner*, 21 July 1921, 1.

[16]EGW to Uriah & Harriet Smith, 15 June 1884.

[17]*RH*, 31 July 1930, 29; *Gleaner*, 3 June 1930, 9.

[18]*Sixty Years*, 84-86; Terri D. Aamodt, *Bold Venture: A History of Walla Walla College* (College Place, WA: Walla Walla College, 1992), 9-21.

[19]Ibid, 291.

[20]*Sixty Years*, 97, 120-121; *1900-1901 Walla Walla City and County Directory*, 240; *Deed Book 64* (p. 264) and *Deed Book 65* (193) (Walla Walla, WA: Walla Walla County Clerk Office, 1897).

8 New Leaders for the Northwest

[1]*RH*, 25 November 1902, 23; Cindy and Florence Stewart, "Spiritual Genetics—The Stewart Family," *How the Faith Was Won Place:* Upper Columbia Conference, 1994 (a camp meeting booklet), 13-14; Ford, 6.

[2]*RH*, 17 June 1880, 394.

[3]*Farmington SDA Church Centennial Booklet*, 1985; *ST*, 2 March 1882, 104; *ST*, 30 March 1882, 152; *ST*, 23 June 1883, 297.

[4]*RH*, 6 September 1934, 21; *SDAEncy*, 555; *RH*, 21 June 1887, 397, *SDA Yearbook*, 1904 53; *SDA Yearbook*, 1915 61.

[5]Alonzo T. Jones to Willie White, 5 November 1883; Alonzo T. Jones to EGW, 5, November 1883.

[6]*ST*, 22 June 1882, 283.

[7]EGW to Uriah and Harriet Smith, 15 June 1884.

[8]*ST*, 22 July 1882, 283.

[9]*RH*, 2 January 1883, 12.

[10]*ST*, 28 June 1883, 297.

[11]*RH*, 18 September 1883, 604; *RH*, 20 November 1883, 731; *ST*, 10 April 1884, 235; Ford, 7.

[12]Alonzo T. Jones to Willie White, 13 April 1884.

[13]*Sixty Years*, 115; *RH*, 19 June 1888, 396; *RH*, 3 July 1894, 424; EGW, *Testimonies to Ministers and Gospel Workers*, 91.

[14]*RH*, 7 October 1884, 635; Ford, 7.

[15]*ST*, 28 August 1884, 527.

[16]*ST*, 19 March 1885, 186.

[17]*ST*, 28 August 1884, 528.

[18]*RH*, 3 January 1882, 16.

[19]*SDAEncy*, 840-842.

[20]*SDAEncy*, 150; Dorothy Minchin-Comm, "Do They Make Women Like Her Anymore?" *Adventist Review*, 3 March 1994, 12- 13.

[21]*ST*, 29 June 1882, 297.

[22]*RH*, 26 July 1881, 76; I. Van Horn to EGW, 1 April 1884.

[23]*ST*, 14 July 1881, 306; Starbuck, 16-18; Zitek, 46-48.

[24]*ST*, 28 July 1881, 331.

[25]*ST*, 13 July 1882, 309; *ST*, 19 July 1883, 321; Starbuck, 32-35; *ST*, 4 January 1883, 9.

[26]*ST*, 12 July 1883, 307-308; *ST*, 16 August 1883, 369; *ST*, 6 September 1883, 405.

[27]*ST*, 4 October 1883, 441; *ST*, 6 December 1883, 549.

[28]*RH*, 1 January 1884, 5; Starbuck, 33-35.

[29]*RH*, 1 January 1884, 5.

[30]*ST*, 27 July 1882, 333; *ST*, 14 September 1882, 405; *ST*, 30 November 1882, 527.

[31]*ST*, 16 February 1882, 81.

[32]*ST*, 29 June 1882, 297.

[33]*ST*, 17 July 1884, 424; EGW to Stephen N. Haskell, 10 June 1884.

[34]*RH*, 12 December 1882, 778; *RH*, 9 January 1883, 28; *ST*, 19 April 1883, 188.

[35]*RH*, 10 July 1879, 23; *ST*, 29 June 1882, 297; *ST*, 19 July 1883, 321.

[36]I. Van Horn to EGW, 1 April 1884.

[37]*RH*, 29 April 1884, 285; EGW to Uriah and Harriet Smith, 15 June 1884; *ST*, 1 May 1884, 266.

[38]*ST*, 3 July 1884, 408; EGW to Uriah and Harriet Smith, 15 June 1884; EGW to Stephen N. Haskell, 10 June 1884.

9 The Crisis of 1884

[1]The Daily Journal, 3 June 1884.

[2]*ST*, 3 July 1884, 408.

[3]EGW to Uriah & Harriet Smith, 15 June 1884.

[4]EGW to Uriah Smith, 27 June 1884.

[5]EGW, T5: 293.

[6]EGW to Uriah & Harriet Smith, 15 June 1884.

[7]EGW to Uriah Smith, Letter 7, 1884.

[8]EGW to Uriah Smith, 27 June 1884.

[9]*General Conference Bulletin*, 1893, 19-20.

[10]EGW to S.N. Haskell, 10 June 1884; *ST*, 17 July 1884, 424.

[11]*ST*, 17 July 1884, 425-431; *ST*, 3 July 1884, 408; *Sixty Years*, 84, 85.

[12]*ST*, 17 July 1884, 424.

[13]*RH*, 15 December 1885, 783; *RH*, 5 November 1889, 697.

10 The West Side

[1]*ST*, 31 July 1884, 459.

[2]*ST*, 14 August 1884, 491.

[3]*Ibid.*, 490; *ST*, 9 October 1884, 602; *RH*, 9 December 1880, 380.

[4]*ST*, 5 February 1885, 91.

[5]*RH*, 27 January 1885, 59; *RH*, 10 March 1885, 156.

[6]*ST*, 26 February 1885, 139.

[7]*ST*, 6 March 1884, 155; *RH*, 29 April 1884, 285; *H*, 19 May 1885, 315; *ST*, 16 July 1885, 427.

[8]*ST*, 16 July 1885, 427.

[9]*Ibid.*; *RH*, 14 June 1887, 382; *H*, 20 October 1885, 651.

[10]*ST*, 29 October 1885, 651; *ST*, 24 December 1885, 775.

[11]*ST*, 1 October 1885, 586; *RH*, 26 January 1886, 60.

[12]Eric B. Hare, *Fulton's Footprints in Fiji* (Boise, ID: Pacific Press Pub. Assoc.), 16, 28, 29, 39-45; *SDA Yearbook*, 1886, 8; *SDAEncy*, 427.

[13]*ST*, 17 July 1884, 426; *ST*, 16 July 1885, 425-427; *ST*, 10 June 1886, 345-346.

[14]*ST*, 1 August 1878; *RH*, 20 October 1885, 651; *RH*, 15 June 1886, 381. North Pacific Conference churches in 1886: Oregon: Beaverton, Coquille, Corvallis, Damascus, East Portland, Newton, Salem, Toledo and West Chahalem; Washington Territory: Carrolton, Lynden, Renton and Vancouver.

[15]*ST*, 26 August 1886, 522; *ST*, 18 November 1886, 698.

[16]*ST*, 12 August 1886, 489; *ST*, 18 November 1886, 698; *ST*, 16 June 1887, 361.

[17]*ST*, 7 April 1887, 218; *RH*, 5 April 1887, 219.

[18]Ibid.; *SDAEncy*, 150-151, 656.

[19]*RH*, 14 June 1887, 382.

[20]*ST*, 23 June 1887, 377; *RH*, 14 June 1887, 382.

[21]*SDA Yearbook*, 1888, 3.

[22]Ibid.; 8; *SDAEncy*, 656; *ST*, 6 July 1888, 408.

[23]*ST*, 17 June 1889, 360; Hare, 39; Zitek, 268; *ST*, 19 May 1890, 302.

[24]*ST*, 17 June 1889, 363; *SDAEncy*, 803, 1005; *RH*, 24 June 1890, 397.

[25]*ST*, 6 July 1888, 409; *RH*, 18 June 1889, 396.

[26]*RH*, 18 October 1887, 652; *ST*, 9 March 1888, 152.

[27]*ST*, 6 July 1888, 408.

[28]*ST*, 21 September 1888; *ST*, 12 October 1888, 619.

[29]*ST*, 17 June 1889, 363.

[30]Ibid., 359-360 & 363; *SDA Yearbook*, 1888, 5.

[31]*SDA Yearbook*, 1886, 57; *RH*, 5 November 1889, 697; *ST*, 11 February 1889, 91; *ST*, 17 June 1889, 362-363. North Pacific Conference churches in 1889: Oregon: Albany, Beaverton, Coquille, Corvallis, Damascus, East Portland, Elk City (Newton), Gravel Ford, Marshfield, Royal, Salem, St. Johns, West Union, Woodburn and Woodland; Washington Territory: Artondale, Carrolton, Ilwaco, Lynden, Maple Valley (Renton), Seattle, Spring Brook (Kent), Tacoma, Vancouver, and Victoria (British Columbia, Canada).

[32]*ST*, 16 July 1885, 427; *RH*, 18 June 1889, 396; *ST*, 30 June 1890, 395; *RH*, 24 June 1890, 397.

[33]*ST*, 2 September 1889, 539; *ST*, 30 June 1890, 395.

[34]*RH*, 17 April 1894, 251.

[35]*ST*, 30 June 1890, 395; *RH*, 24 June 1890, 397; *SDAEncy*, 929; *RH*, 14 March 1935; Zitek, 269.

[36]*SDA Yearbook*, 1890, 8; *RH*, 17 July 1883, 461; *ST*, 17 July 1884, 426; *RH*, 15 June 1886, 381; *RH*, 14 June 1887, 382; *ST*, 6 July 1888, 408; *ST*, 17 June 1889, 363.

[37]*RH*, 14 March 1935, 22.

[38]*RH*, 7 October 1890, 620; *RH*, 14 July 1891, 442; *SDA Yearbook*, 1888, 10.

11 Puget Sound

[1]Schwantes, 192-97; Murray & Rosa Morgan, *South on the Sound* (Woodland Hills, Calif.: Windsor Publishing, 1984), 39-69; James R. Warren, *King County and Her Queen City: Seattle* (Woodland Hills, CA: Windsor Publishing, 1981), 68-87.

[2]*RH*, 26 July 1881, 76; *ST*, 15 December 1881, 560.

[3]*ST*, 30 November 1882, 536-537; *RH*, 12 December 1882, 778; *RH*, 9 January 1883, 28.

[4]*ST*, 4 January 1883, 9.

[5]*A Few Facts about Seattle* (Seattle, WA: Arthur C. Jackson, 1898); Schwantes, 192.

[6]*Seattle Post-Intelligencer*, 22 June 1886; *ST*, 22 July 1886, 442.

[7]*RH*, 7 September 1886, 571; *RH*, 21 September 1886, 604; *ST*, 30 September 1886, 601.

[8]*ST*, 17 February 1887, 106; *ST*, 24 March 1887, 186; *ST*, 15 September 1887, 570.

[9]*ST*, 6 October 1887, 618; *ST*, 20 October 1887, 634.

[10]*RH*, 21 September 1886, 604; *RH*, 5 April 1887, 219; *ST*, 5 August 1889, 474; *ST*, 30 June 1890, 395; SDAEncy, 164-165.

[11]*RH*, 6 January 1891, 11; *RH*, 14 June 1891, 442.

[12]*General Conference Bulletin*, 1893, 318; *SDAEncy*, 165.

[13]*ST*, 18 February 1889, 107; *RH*, 27 August 1889, 540.

[14]*ST*, 26 October 1888, 650; *RH*, 12 October 1886, 635; *RH*, 1 July 1890, 413.

[15]*RH*, 3 November 1896, 704.

[16]*SDAEncy*, 1391; *ST*, 5 August 1889, 474-475.

[17]*RH*, 10 April 1894, 237.

[18]Eric B. Hare, *Fulton's Footprints in Fiji* (Boise, ID: Pacific Press Pub. Assoc., 1985), 17-45.

[19]*RH*, 14 July 1891, 442.

[20]*RH*, 6 September 1892, 570; *Gleaner*, 25 April 1933, 1- 2.

[21]*RH*, 1 July 1902, 18; *General Conference Bulletin*, 1903, 48; *Gleaner*, 18 May 1916, 6.

12 The Inland Empire

[1]John Faley, *The Inland Empire Unfolding Years, 1879-1929* (Seattle, WA: University of Washington Press, 1986), xi-xii.

[2]*ST*, 2 July 1885, 411; *RH*, 15 December 1885, 783; *SDA Yearbook*, 1883, 16; *SDAEncy*, 840. Upper Columbia Conference churches in 1885: Dayton, Echo, Farmington, Goldendale, Lostine, Milton, Pataha and Walla Walla.

[3]*RH*, 18 November 1926, 22; *Gleaner*, 2 November 1926, 10.

[4]*SDAEncy*, 1434; *RH*, 9 September 1875, 78; *RH*, 15 December 1885, 783.

[5]*ST*, 19 March 1885, 186; *ST*,16 April 1885, 251.

[6]*ST*, 23 April 1885, 271; *ST*, 26 June 1885, 394.

[7]*ST*, 25 June 1885, 394.

[8]*ST*, 2 July 1885, 411.

[9]*SDA Yearbook*, 1886, 57; *ST*, 24 June 1886, 377.

[10]*ST*, 16 July 1885, 427; *ST*, 3 September 1885, 538.

[11]*RH*, 23 February 1886, 126; *RH*, 18 February 1886, 106; *RH*, 5 August 1926, 22; *SDAEncy*, 966-967.

[12]Edwards, 55-64; 272-273; Schwantes, 197-198.

[13]Ford, 8-9; *RH*, 17 May 1887, 316; *RH*, 3 July 1888, 428; *Spokane Central SDA Church Centennial Booklet*; Edwards, 156.

[14]*ST*, 25 August 1887, 521; *RH*, 13 September 1887, 587; *RH*, 3 July 1888, 428; *ST*, 15 April 1889, 235; *RH*, 17 January 1888, 44.

[15]*SDAEncy*, 1367; *SDA Yearbook*, 1888, 6. Upper Columbia Conference ordained ministers in 1888: J. Bartlett, Henry Decker, Daniel T. Fero and James W. Scoles.

[16]*RH*, 3 July 1888, 428; *RH*, 14 July 1891, 441- 442; *RH*, 15 June 1897, 381; *RH*, 2 May 1907, 20; *RH*, 30 March 1933, 22; *SDAEncy*, 43; *RH*, 16 September 1937, 22. Early Upper Columbia Conference ministerial recruits included: Elmer E. Andross, Albert G. Christiansen, Alonzo T. Jones, C. N. Martin, Henry W. Oliver, D. E. Scoles, Will W. Steward, Edwin L. Stewart.

[17]*RH*, 19 June 1888, 396-397.

[18]*ST*, 22 June 1888, 375; *SDAEncy*, 1194. The four churches include: Alba, Oregon; Medical Lake, Moscow and Spokane Falls.

[19]*ST*, 31 August 1888, 538; *ST*, 7 September 1888, 555; *ST*, 15 April 1889, 235.

[20]*SDA Yearbook*, 1888, 9-10; *SDA Yearbook*, 1889, 60-61; *SDAEncy*, 202-203; *RH*, 12 March 1936, 21; Arthur W. Spalding, *Footprints of the Pioneers* (Washington, DC: Review and Herald Pub. Assoc., 1947), 209-218.

[21]*ST*, 17 June 1889, 359; *ST*, 15 July 1889, 427; *RH*, 5 November 1889, 697. Upper Columbia Conference churches in 1889: Alba, Boise City, Dayton, Echo (Oregon), Farmington, Franklin (Idaho), Garfield, Heppner, Highland Valley (Idaho), Lostine, Medical Lake, Milton, Moscow, Pataha, Spokane Falls, and Walla Walla.

[22]Aamodt, 9-17; W. W. Prescott to O. A. Olsen, 25 September 1890; Henry W. Decker to O. A. Olsen, 10 November 1890; Dan T. Jones to O. A. Olsen, 7 June 1891; Dan T. Jones to O. A. Olsen, 6 January 1892.

[23]*RH*, 15 December 1885, 783; *RH*, 11 July 1893, 444.

[24]Aamodt, 11-19; Dan T. Jones to O. A. Olsen, 6 January 1892.

[25]*SDAEncy*, 929 & 1305; 1893 *General Conference Bulletin*, 21 February 1813, 9; 1893, 9; *RH*, 18 November 1926, 22.

[26]Aamodt, 17; *Sixty Years*, 19.

[27]Faley, 14; Schwantes, 160.

[28]*RH*, 23 June 1896, 396.

[29]*The Reaper* (Upper Columbia Conference magazine), 8 March 1899, 4. Leading towns and cities in the Upper Columbia Conference today with a church in 1900 (x): Coeur D'Alene, Ellensburg, Hermiston, Lewiston-Clarkston (x), Moscow-Pullman (x), Moses Lake, Pendleton, Spokane (x), Tri-cities, Yakima [North Yakima] (x), Walla Walla (x) and Wentachee (x).

[30]Monte Sahlin, Charles Taylor, and F. Donald Yost, *Global Mission Databook 1990* (Hagerstown, Maryland: Review and Herald Pub. Assoc., 1991), 91-98; *North American Division Summary of Progress, Fourth Quarter, 1989* (Place: Archives & Statistics of General Conference of SDA), 2-4.

13 Father and Son

[1]Schwantes, 86; Mattes, 47-55.

[2]*Milton Eagle*, March 1897; Gilbert, 97-98; Barbara Westphal, *These Fords Still Run* (Mountain View, CA: Pacific Press Pub. Assoc., 1962), 7-9.

[3]Ninevah Ford, "Recollections of Ninevah Ford" (33-page manuscript at

the Bancroft Library, University of California, Berkeley, Calif., n.d.); Mattes, 49-50.

[4]*Walla Walla Union*, 26 December 1948.

[5]*Gleaner*, 18 February 1930, 12; *Milton Eagle*, March 1897.

[6]*Sixty Years*, 54; Gilbert, 456; *Milton Eagle*, March 1897; William D. Fenton, "Political History of Oregon From 1865 to 1876," *Oregon Historical Quarterly*, 3, 1902, 59-61.

[7]"Ninevah Ford Had His Way about Bridges," *Walla Walla Union Bulletin* (Pemrose Memorial Library, Whitman College, Walla Walla, WA, n.d.).

[8]J. Orin Oliphant, ed., "Minutes West Union Baptist Church," *Oregon Historical Quarterly* 36, 1935, 247- 257.

[9]Church Record Book, 13 February 1875, 2.

[10]*Gleaner*, 18 February 1930, 12.

[11]Alvin M. Josephy, *Nez Perce Country: National Park Handbook* (Washington, DC: National Park Service, 1983), 97-152.

[12]*Gleaner*, 18 February 1930, 12; Ford, *SEH*, 7.

[13]*Sixty Years*, 77-78; Ford, 7; *Walla Walla Union*, 5 March 1881.

[14]Church Record Book, 2 July 1881, minutes of the meetings, 8.

[15]Ford, 7-8; *RH*, 18 September 1883, 604; *ST*, 28 August 1884, 527; *RH*, 7 October 1884, 635.

[16]Ford, 8; *R.L. Polk Inland Empire Directory*, 1885.

[17]Ford, 8-12; *RH*, 17 May 1898, 320.

[18]Ford, 12; 1900 *General Conference Bulletin*, fourth quarter, 213; *SDA Yearbook*, 1906, 61; *SDA Yearbook*, 1910, 197.

[19]*Gleaner*, 18 February 1930, 12.

14 Snake River Adventism

[1]Robert Famighetti, ed., *The World Almanac and Book of Facts* (Mahwah, NJ: Funk & Wagnalls, 1993), 360.

[2]Schwantes, 106.

[3]Carlos A. Schwantes, *In Mountain Shadows: A History of Idaho* (Lincoln, NE: University of Nebraska Press, 1991), 116-117.

[4]*ST*, 9, October 1884, 602.

[5]*ST*, 28 August 1884, 527.

[6]*ST*, 9 October 1884, 602; *ST*, 2 July 1885, 411.

[7]*ST*, 24 June 1886, 377; *ST*, 15 July 1886, 425; *RH*, 18 February 1886, 106; *RH*, 23 February 1886, 126; *RH*, 21 June 1887, 396; *RH*, 13 July 1886, 444; *RH*, 5 August 1926, 22.

[8]*The History of the Boise SDA Church* n.p. (n.p. circa), 5-6.

[9]*SDAEncy*, 555; Schwantes, 244-248.

[10]Harry Orchard, *Harry Orchard: The Man God Made Again* (Nashville, TN: Southen Pub. Assoc. 1952), 142.

[11]Ibid., 143- 147.

[12]*RH*, 14 August 1888, 524.

[13]*ST*, 1 September 1887, 542; *ST*, 17 February 1888, 107; *ST*, 18 August 1890, 456.

[14]*RH*, 5 January 1892, 13.

[15]*RH*, 17 April 1894, 250.

[16]*RH*, 17 December 1895, 812.

[17]*Gleaner*, 7 August 1907, 3; SDA Yearbook, 1926, 60.

[18]*ST*, 3 September 1885, 538; Mr. & Mrs. Leonard LaFountaine interview by author (17 April 1990); *ST*, 3, July 1884, 410; *RH*, 1 August 1893, 490. Early Adventist work in the portion of eastern Oregon that is in the Idaho Conference today: Isaac Van Horn conducted tent meetings in La Grande in 1875 (*RH*, 9 September 1875, 78). William Raymond held meetings in Cove and Powder River Valley in 1879 (*RH*, 1 May 1879, 142). In 1880 several Adventists lived in the Grande Ronde Valley (*RH*, 15 July 1880, 61). Henry Decker and William Raymond held tent meetings in Union and Summerville in 1885 (*ST*, 16 July 1885, 427; *ST*, 3 September 1885, 538). Henry Decker held tent meetings in Prairie City in the John Day Valley in 1888 (*ST*, 31 August 1888, 538). Will W. Steward held meetings at Alder in Wallowa County in 1890, and in Bear Creek schoolhouse and Lostine in the same county during the winter of 1890-1891. In March, he and D. E. Scoles organized a church in Lostine (*RH*, 12 May 1891, 299). During the summer of 1891, Will W. Steward and D. E. Scoles held tent meetings in Enterprise (*RH*, 1 September 1891, 555; *RH*, 9 February 1892, 92). During the winter of 1891-1892, D. E. Scoles held meetings in Joseph, Oregon (*RH*, 3 May 1892, 284).

[19]*RH*, 25 February 1896, 124-125.

[20]Johnson, "Adventism in Pacific . . ." 104-105; *SDAEncy*, 554.

[21]*RH*, 25 January 1898, 64.

[22]Johnson, "Adventism in Pacific . . ." 91-93.

[23]North Pacific Union Conference, 1992 *Church Growth Report*. Church Growth Report (Place: North Pacific Union Conference, 1992).

15 Reading, Writing, and Arithmetic

[1]EGW, T3:160.

[2]*SDAEncy*, 37-38; Schwarz, *Light Bearers to the Remnant* (Mountain View,

CA: Pacific Press Pub. Assoc., 1979), 127-131; Gilbert M. Valentine, *The Shaping of Adventism* (Berrien Springs, MI: Andrews University Press, 1992), 23-37.

[3]*SDAEncy*, 72-73 & 947.

[4]*RH*, 14 December 1886, 784; *RH*, 15 June 1886, 381; *RH*, 22 June 1886, 397; SDA Yearbook, 1889, 122.

[5]*RH*, 15 June 1886, 381.

[6]*ST*, 22 June 1882, 283, 285.

[7]*ST*, 24 June 1886, 377; *Sixty Years*, 84-85.

[8]Mrs. Bob Howard, "Academy Pioneers Secondary Education," *Pioneer Trails* (Place: Umatilla County Historical Society Journal, March, 1977), 3; *Sixty Years*, 84-86; Mildred Searcey, *Way Back When* (Pendleton, OR: East Oregonian Pub. Co., 1972), 151; Aamodt, 9-11; *ST*, 17 February 1888, 107; *ST*, 22 June 1888, 375; *ST*, 27 July 1888, 458; *Milton Academy Catalogue*, 1890, 5-10; Claude Conard to Clara Rogers-Wilson, 14 June 1951.

[9]*Milton Academy Catalogue*, 1890, 6.

[10]*Sixty Years*, 81-85; *RH*, 15 June 1886, 381; Starbuck, 43-44; *Gleaner*, 23 May 1966, 10; *SDA Yearbook*, 1889, 122; *ST*, 9 March 1888, 153; *ST*, 29 June 1888, 391.

[11]*North Pacific Academy Calendar*, 1889, 6; *ST*, 12 October 1888, 619.

[12]*ST*, 12 October 1888, 619.

[13]*ST*, 17 June 1889, 363.

[14]*RH*, 24 June 1890, 397.

[15]Aamodt, 10-12; *Sixty Years*, 86.

[16]EGW to John E. Graham, 14 July 1890.

[17]*RH*, 11 November 1890, 698.

[18]*Milton Eagle*, 9 May 1890, 1.

[19]Aamodt, 9-21; *RH*, 10 January 1893, 29; 1893 *General Conference Bulletin*, 1893, 353-354.

[20]Sixty Years, 76, 83, 84; Dennis Casper interview by author, 1992; *RH*, 3 November 1977, 4-6; *Gleaner*, 30 May 1933, 7; *RH*, 6 January 1891, 11; 1891 *General Conference Bulletin*, 1891, 24.

[21]Schwarz, 204-205.

[22]Washington Conference Academies: *SDAEncy*, 76-77 & 293; *SDA Yearbook*, 1905, 100; 1915; 1916; Oregon Conference Academies: *SDAEncy*, 293, 688, 796, 1008; *Gleaner*, 10 January 1907, 3-4; *SDA Yearbook*, 1920, 85; 1930, 67; *Gleaner*, 5 August 920, 7; Upper Columbia Conference Academies: *SDAEncy*, 1366, 1367 & 1389; Lalia Boone, *From A to Z in Latah County, Idaho* (n.p.: 1983), 100; *Gleaner*, 19 October 1910, 5; *Gleaner*, 21 September

1910, 2; Idaho and Montana Conference Academies: *SDAEncy*, 432, 828; *Gleaner*, 18 August 1909, 4-5. The following is a list of academies that have operated in the Pacific Northwest grouped by conferences. Washington Conference: Forest Home Academy in Mount Vernon (1904-1915); Auburn Adventist Academy in Auburn (1919-present). Oregon Conference: Columbia Academy near Battle Ground, Washington (1903-present); Laurelwood Academy near Gaston (1904-1985); Royal Academy in Cottage Grove (1906-for several years); Sutherlin Academy near Roseburg (1920s & early 1930s); Portland Adventist Academy (1939-present); and Milo Academy near Canyonville (1955-present). Upper Columbia Conference: Kettle Falls Academy, Washington (1897-1904); Berean Industrial School near Wenatchee (1908-1909); Yakima Valley Intermediate Academy in Yakima (1908-1915); Thatuna Academy near Viola, Idaho (1908-1915); Yakima Valley Academy in Granger (1921-1945); Upper Columbia Academy (1945-present); Walla Walla Valley Academy (became separate from the college in 1964-present). Montana Conference: Montana Intermediate School (Mount Ellis Academy) in Bozeman (1902-present). Idaho Conference: Ames Industrial School in Eagle (1909-mid 1910s); Gem State Academy (1919-present).

16 Conrad Hall—The Rest of the Story

[1]Ruth Conard, *Across the Plains—And Beyond* (Washington, DC: Review and Herald Pub. Assoc., n.d.), 19-21, 32-34; Mattes, 345-346; *Gleaner*, 5 January 1910, 7-8.

[2]Conard, 85-94, 124-128, 135-150.

[3]Ibid., 151-177; *Gleaner*, 5 January 1910, 7-8.

[4]Conard, 179-224; *Gleaner*, 5 January 1910, 7-8; *Sixty Years*, 41, 93, 361 & 374.

[5]Johnson, *"Adventism in Pacific . . ."*, 119.

17 Big Sky Country

[1]Michael Malone, Richard B. Roeder, William L. Lang, *Montana: A History of Two Centuries* (Seattle, WA: University of Washington Press, 1976), 64-71.

[2]Ibid., 145-158, 232-235; Famighetti, 360.

[3]*SDAEncy*, 1367; *RH*, 14 December 1886, 784.

[4]*RH*, 7 August 1888, 508; *RH*, 11 December 1888, 779.

[5]*RH*, 23 July 1889, 475-476; *RH*, 17 September 1889, 587.

[6]*RH*, 13 March 1930, 29; *RH*, 24 June 1890, 396; *RH*, 14 October

1890, 632-633.

[7]*RH*, 3 November 1891, 684.

[8]Ibid., 684; *RH*, 19 July 1892, 461- 462.

[9]*RH*, 19 July 1892, 461.

[10]*RH*, 21 February 1893, 124.

[11]*RH*, 14 July 1891, 441; *RH*, 30 March 1933, 22.

[12]*ST*, 4 February 1889, 78; *RH*, 19 July 1892, 460; Dan T. Jones to O. A. Olsen, 30 June 1892; Dan T. Jones to O. A. Olsen, 31 July 1892.

[13]Dan T. Jones to O. A. Olsen, 11 September 1892; Dan T. Jones to O. A. Olsen, 22 September 1892; *General Conference Bulletin*, 1893, 319.

[14]EGW, *Testimonies to Ministers*, 58-62.

[15]A. W. Stanton, *The Loud Cry of the Third Angel's Message* (1893); EGW, *Testimonies to Ministers*, 521.

[16]Ibid., 32-33.

[17]Ibid. 22-23.

[18]*General Conference Bulletin*, 1893, 319; *RH*, 24 April 1930, p 29; *SDAEncy*, 1403.

[19]*RH*, 4 July 1893, 428; *RH*, 15 August 1893, 522; *RH*, 22 August 1893, 537; *RH*, 24 October 1893, 670; *RH*, 14 November 1893, 720.

[20]*RH*, 10 July 1894, 444.

[21]*General Conference Bulletin*, 1895, 253; *SDAEncy*, 293, 576.

[22]RH 23 January 1894, 60; *SDAEncy*, 821-822; *RH*, 7 May 1895, 301; *General Conference Bulletin*, 1895, 253.

[23]*RH*, 10 September 1895, 588.

[24]*RH*, 3 December 1895, 781.

[25]*RH*, 10 September 1895, 588.

[26]*RH*, 11 February 1896, 92.

[27]*RH*, 6 September 1898, 578; *RH*, 8 November 1898, 720; *SDAEncy*, 1425.

[28] *Church Growth Report*. (Place: North Pacific Union Conference, 1992).

18 The Story Uncle Arthur Got Wrong

[1]*RH*, 3 July 1894, 424-425.

[2]Arthur S. Maxwell, *Uncle Arthur's Bedtime Stories*, Vol. 5 (Washington, DC: Review and Herald Pub. Assoc., 1951), 59-61.

[3]*Sixty Years*, 107.

[4]*RH*, 3 July 1894, 424-425.

19 Kellogg's Health System/Northwest

[1]Schwarz, 108-117, 206; *SDAEncy*, 110-112.

[2]Schwarz, John Harvey Kellogg, M.D., (Nashville, TN: Southen Pub. Assoc. 1970), 113, 116-128; *SDAEncy*, 648-649.

[3]Schwarz, *Kellogg*, 75-76.

[4]Ibid., 137-138, 159, 187-189.

[5]Starbuck, 41; *Gleaner*, 6 September 1993, 4.

[6]*RH*, 31 July 1894, 493.

[7]Starbuck, 42; *SDAEncy*, 1007; *Gleaner*, 31 July 1993, 4-6.

[8]Schwarz, *Kellogg*, 157-173; Gary Land, ed., *Adventism in America* (Grand Rapids, MI.: Eerdmans Pub. Co., 1986), 111.

[9]*RH*, 17 May 1898, 320; *RH*, 10 May 1898, 305; *RH*, 1 August 1899, 497.

[10]*SDAEncy*, 269.

[11]*Sixty Years*, 107, 126, 362.

[12]*RH*, 29 July 1902, 22-23; Jonathan Edwards, 156.

[13]SDA Yearbook, 1905, 119; *Sixty Years*, 153-154; *Gleaner*, 16 November 1905, 20.

[14]*R. L. Polk Walla Walla and County Directory* (Seattle, WA: R. L. Polk Co., 1905), 162.

[15]*Sixty Years*, 153-155.

[16]*SDAEncy*, 1389.

[17]*Gleaner*, 25 September 1907, 6.

[18]Schwarz, *Kellogg*, 282-297.

[19]SDA *Yearbooks,* 1904, 97; 1905, 118; 1908, 180; 1909, 186, 192, 193; 1911, 187; 1913, 200; *Gleaner*, 1 November 1906, 16 October 1907, 3; 29 July 1908, 2; Floyd O. Rittenhouse, "The Story of Seventh-day Adventists in Montana" (51-page paper on the history of the Montana Conference), January, 1988, 26.

20 The Germans and Scandinavians

[1]Schwantes, 124-125, 188.

[2]Ibid., 258.

[3]Ibid., 125.

[4]General Conference Bulletin, 1893, 318; *RH*, 31 July 1894, 492.

[5]Schwantes, 188.

[6]Olsen, 345-348.

[7]Lewis Harrison Christian, *Sons of the North* (Mountain View, CA: Pacific

Press Pub. Assoc., 1942), 137.

[8]*ST*, 9 June 1887, 351.

[9]*RH*, 8 May 1900, 301.

[10]*General Conference Bulletin*, 1893, 319; Claude Conard to Clara Rogers-Wilson, 14 June 1951; *Milton Academy Catalogue*, 1890, 11.

[11]*RH*, 3 July 1894, 425.

[12]*RH*, 28 June 1898, 414; *RH*, 29 May 1900, 348; *General Conference Bulletin*, 1900, 210, 213. Scandinavian churches in the Northwest: Ballard, Bellingham, Everett, Ferndale, Spokane & Tacoma in Washington. Lebanon, Monitor, Portland in Oregon.

[13]Olsen, 399-403.

[14]*General Conference Bulletin*, 1889, 121.

[15]SDA Yearbook, 1889, 32; 1890, 10; *ST*, 17 June 1889, 360; *RH*, 14 July 1891, 442.

[16]*RH*, 3 June 1890, 348; *RH*, 16 June 1891, 381.

[17]*RH*, 14 July 1891, 441.

[18]*General Conference Bulletin*, 1893, 319.

[19]*RH*, 7 March 1893, 157.

[20]*RH*, 11 July 1893, 444; *Sixty Years*, 169; Aamodt, 151; *Gleaner*, 3 February 1942, 5.

[21]Richard D. Scheuerman, *Pilgrims on the Earth* (Fairfield, WA: Ye Galleon Press, 1976), 113; Grace L. Ochs, *Up from the Volga* (Nashville, TN: Southen Pub. Assoc. 1969), 45-50.

[22]Henry L. Rudy interview by author, 1979; Alec Rudy interview by author, 1979.

[23]Church Record Book, Wilcox German SDA Church, 1915, 20.

[24]*Gleaner*, 13 December 1906, 6. German SDA churches in the Northwest: College Place, Endicott, Farmington, Spokane, Wilcox in Washington. Marsh, Billings in Montana. West Union in Oregon. Dalton (Hayden) in Idaho.

[25]Olsen, 690-691.

21 Evangelism in the Wild West

[1]*Famighetti*, ed., 534-535.

[2]*Gleaner*, 1 April 1991, 10; *Gleaner*, 22 January 1908, 7; *Gleaner*, 8 May 1906; *Gleaner*, 29 January 1908, 7; *Gleaner*, 18 December 1907, 8.

[3]*RH*, 26 August 1875, 62; Johnson, *"Adventism in Pacific . . .,"*, 70-71.

[4]*RH*, 16 June 1896, 380.

[5]*RH*, 3 May 1892, 284.

[6]*RH*, 14 September 1897, 587.

[7]*RH*, 22 December 1891, 796.
[8]*RH*, 2 December 1890, 747.
[9]*Athena Press*, 21 July 1893.
[10]*Athena Press*, 4 August 1893.
[11]*Athena Press*, 11 August 1893.
[12]*Athena Press*, 18 August 1893.
[13]*Athena Press*, 2, September 1893.
[14]*Athena Press*, 9 September 1893.
[15]*Athena Press*, 15 September 1893.
[16]*Athena Press*, 22 September 1893.

22 Frontier Religion

[1]Famighetti, ed., 426; *SDAEncy* (give most impportant ones); *ST*, 9 September 1875; *SDA Yearbook*, 1886, 57; *General Conference Bulletin* (4th quarter), 1900, 198.

The Spread of Sabbatarian Adventism in the United States

Established States
Adventist (Sabbatarian) ministers first entered these states
more than 20 years after statehood.

State	Date of State-hood	SDA Minister Arrives	SDA Membership		
			1875	1885	1900
Alabama	1819	1876			240
Arkansas	1836	1877			320
Atlantic Conference:					897
Delaware	1787	1870s			
Dist. Columbia					
Maryland	1788	1851			
New Jersey	1787	1874			
Florida	1845	1883			639
Georgia	1788	1876			206

State	Date of Statehood	SDA Minister Arrives	SDA Membership		
			1875	1885	1900
Kentucky/Tennessee:				232	921
Kentucky	1792	1871			
Tennessee	1796	1871			
Illinois	1818	1850	350	729	1,760
Indiana	1816	1849	158	920	2,194
Louisiana	1812	1880s			144
Maine	1820	1840s	266	416	681
Mississippi	1817	1880s			110
Missouri	1821	1858	173	563	2,615
New England Conf.:			350	561	1,587
Connecticut	1788	1840s			
Massachusetts	1788	1840s			
New Hampshire	1788	1840s			
Rhode Island	1790	1840s			
New York/Penn.:			591		
New York	1788	1840s		766	1,749
Pennsylvania	1787	1851		525	1,896
North Carolina	1789	1876			164
Ohio	1803	1851	266	944	2,560
South Carolina	1788	1893			45
Texas	1845	1876		300	1,350
Vermont	1791	1840s	323	456	632
Virginia	1788	1876		105	300

Frontier or semi-frontier states
Adventist (Sabbatarian) ministers first entered these regions

as territories or within 20 years of statehood

State	Date of State-hood	SDA Minister Arrives	SDA Membership		
			1875	1885	1900
Alaska	1959	1901			
California Conf.:			450	1,587	4,485
Arizona	1912	1890			
California	1850	1868			
Nevada	1864	1877			
Utah	1896	1889			
Hawaii	1959	1885			
Colorado:				195	2,325
Colorado	1876	1873			
New Mexico	1912	1890s			
Wyoming	1890	1890s			
Dakota:				488	1,799
North Dakota	1889	1870s			
South Dakota	1889	1874			
Iowa/Nebraska:			884		
Iowa	1846	1856		1,460	4,055
Nebraska	1867	1870		500	2,605
Kansas	1861	1869	173	1,313	3,420
Michigan	1837	1849	2,226	3,809	7,722
Minnesota	1858	1860	700	1,488	3,250
Montana	1889	1888			479
Oklahoma	1907	1892			915
North Pacific Conf.:				237	2405
Western Oregon	1859	1876			
Western WA	1889	1882			

State	Date of State-hood	SDA Minister Arrives	SDA Membership		
			1875	1885	1900
Upper Columbia Conf.:				180	1,400
Eastern Oregon	1859	1874			
Eastern WA	1889	1874			
Idaho	1890	1884			
Wisconsin	1848	1852	933	1,525	3,763
West Virginia	1863	1879			375

[2]Famighetti, ed., 360-361. Population of the established states in 1900: 58,323,000; population of the frontier or semi-frontier states in 1900: 17,889,000.

[3]1900 *General Conference Bulletin*, 1900 (fourth quarter) 198; Famighetti, ed., 360-361.

[4]Famighetti, ed., 426; *SDAEncy*, 17, 57, 290-291, 554, 821, 848, 878, 911, 1222-1224, 1366. The regions of the United States that Adventism entered as territories: Alaska, Arizona, Colorado, Hawaii, Idaho, Montana, New Mexico, North Dakota, Oklahoma, South Dakota, Utah, Washington.